Professional
Development
for *Successful*
Classrooms

Differentiating the Curriculum for Gifted Learners

Wendy Conklin, M.A.
and Shelly Frei

SHELL EDUCATION

Differentiating the Curriculum for Gifted Learners

Editor
Maria Elvira Kessler, M.A.

Project Manager
Maria Elvira Kessler, M.A.

Editor-in-Chief
Sharon Coan, M.S.Ed.

Creative Director
Lee Aucoin

Cover Design
Lee Aucoin
Lesley Palmer

Imaging
Phil Garcia
Don Tran

Publisher
Corinne Burton, M.A.Ed.

Shell Education

5301 Oceanus Drive

Huntington Beach, CA 92649-1030

www.shelleducation.com

ISBN-978-1-4258-0372-8

©2007 Shell Education
Reprinted 2009
Made in U.S.A.

Table of Contents

Table of Contents (cont.)

Table of Contents *(cont.)*

Table of Contents *(cont.)*

Introduction

The education of gifted students is a complicated topic. Many teachers shy away from talking about it because the subject intimidates them and possibly raises many questions. Some of the following reservations could be questions that you or your colleagues have considered:

- What does it mean for a child to be "gifted"?
- How are gifted students different from mainstream students?
- Why do gifted children need special services in our schools?
- How does a gifted educational program differ from mainstream education?
- What are the best ways to differentiate instruction for gifted students?
- How should curriculum be taught to students who are identified as gifted?
- If gifted children are so bright, shouldn't they just be able to make it on their own?

This book will take the mystery out of teaching gifted children by addressing effective research-supported ways to differentiate instruction, as well as how curriculum can be extended, accelerated, and enriched for gifted children. It discusses how a teacher can correctly identify gifted students. This book explores the reasons why gifted students should be serviced in our schools and some of the most effective ways to accomplish this.

Within this book you will also find:

- A vocabulary review and glossary that will help teachers identify the most important terminology surrounding gifted education

- Strategies for identifying gifted students, modifying content, and differentiating instruction in a classroom with gifted students

- Post-chapter reflection questions to help the reader reflect on how to apply the new knowledge learned

- Additional resources at the end of each chapter with professional readings for further research

This book is divided into ten chapters. **Chapter 1** explains what the word "gifted" means, as well as reasons for having gifted programming in schools. Characteristics of gifted children are discussed in **Chapter 2**. Teachers will learn ways to make their classrooms great learning environments through differentiation for gifted children in **Chapter 3**. **Chapter 4** shows ways to compact the curriculum for students who have mastered most of the content. Questioning techniques involving Bloom's Taxonomy are discussed in **Chapter 5**. **Chapter 6** highlights Sandra Kaplan's model of making curriculum more challenging by adding depth and complexity. Ways to write tiered lesson plans are showcased in **Chapter 7**. **Chapter 8** shows teachers how to manage individualized learning contracts with students in their classrooms. Ways to incorporate creative problem solving is dealt with in **Chapter 9**. Finally, **Chapter 10** helps teachers celebrate the varied ways that gifted children are intelligent by designing lessons using Howard Gardner's Multiple Intelligences theory.

Vocabulary Review

Education is notorious for its jargon. Many of the terms specific to the topic of gifted education are used in this book. Some of the terms directly relate to the strategies recommended in this book for teachers of gifted students. In order to have a better understanding of these particular terms, complete the vocabulary review below. Before you read on in the book, note your initial definition in the first column. Then, when you have finished reading the book, note your final definition of each term, and see whether your definitions have changed. You will also find the definition of each of these terms in the Glossary.

Term	My First Definition	My Final Definition
acceleration		
analysis		
application		
Bloom's Taxonomy of Cognitive Thought		
bodily/kinesthetic intelligence		
complexity		
comprehension		
content		
creative problem solving		

Term	My First Definition	My Final Definition
curriculum compacting		
depth		
differentiation		
enrichment		
evaluation		
gifted and talented		
giftedness		
individualized learning contracts		
interpersonal intelligence		
intrapersonal intelligence		
knowledge		
logical/mathematical intelligence		

Term	My First Definition	My Final Definition
Multiple Intelligences Model		
musical/rhythmic intelligence		
naturalist intelligence		
problem solving		
process		
product		
scaffolding		
synthesis		
tiered assignments		
verbal/linguistic intelligence		
visual/spatial intelligence		

Understanding Gifted Learners

Imagine this scenario: Just before school starts in August, your principal informs you that your class will have several gifted children in it. He believes that because you are a competent teacher, you will also be a great teacher for gifted children. He informs you that these bright young children can even be the tutors and special helpers for those who are struggling in your class.

This scenario may cause teachers to panic. One common fear that teachers have about teaching gifted children is that they may know more than they do about certain topics like the solar system and George Washington. Another common fear is that the teacher won't know how to extend and adapt content for these advanced students. Teachers may envision students finishing their work far ahead of the rest of the class and constantly asking, "What do I do now?" Teachers may wonder how they can possibly teach their expected content to all of their students with extra instruction for struggling students and extension of materials for gifted students. If this scenario becomes reality for you, you must first seek an understanding of the term "gifted." It is also very important to become informed about and recognize common misconceptions about gifted students.

What Does "Gifted" Mean?

As you search to understand what it means to be a gifted student, it is quite possible that you will find many different definitions for the term "gifted." It seems as though everybody has their own ideas about giftedness. This, in turn, affects decisions about what should be done for gifted children. "Unfortunately, there are many misconceptions of the term, all of which become deterrents to understanding and catering to the needs of children identified as gifted" ("Giftedness and the Gifted," 1990, p. 2). The topic of deciding which children are gifted and how to best educate these students can sometimes cause controversy between those who provide funds, those who provide state and district guidelines for the education of gifted students, administrators, teachers, parents, and even the students themselves. Therefore, it is essential that educators have a research-based understanding of the term "gifted" before they begin to make decisions about how to educate their gifted students.

How Researchers Define "Gifted"

The quest to define giftedness has changed throughout the last century. In the past, the term giftedness was closely associated with IQ. Lewis Terman, a professor at Stanford University in the early 20th century, is credited as the first person to use the term "gifted child." He is thought of as the "father" of the movement for gifted education because he developed the first test to measure intelligence in 1916, although efforts to educate gifted students date back as far as 1868 (NAGC, 2005a). He called it the Intelligence Quotient test, or IQ test. His IQ test focused heavily upon analytical skills and memory. At first, Terman believed that the intelligence of a person alone defined their giftedness. It is an idea that still circulates today. Nowadays, if you search "IQ test" on an Internet search engine, you will find a wide variety of tests that "will notify you" of your intelligence quotient, often for a fee. However, after many years of research, Terman concluded that personality had as much to do with giftedness as IQ. He believed that a gifted person needed emotional and social confidence, as well as a drive to be successful (NAGC, 2005a).

In 1971, the Marland Report to Congress outlined six areas of giftedness, which included general ability, specific academic aptitude, creative or productive thinking, leadership ability, visual and performing arts, and psychomotor ability. These six areas are commonly utilized and discussed throughout research and educational papers about teaching gifted students, although psychomotor ability has since been excluded from the official federal definition (NAGC, 2005a).

Various researchers since Terman have put forth their contributions to the ever-changing perceptions of the meaning of the term gifted. Renzulli defines a gifted person by the following traits: above average, though not necessarily superior, general ability; a high level of task commitment; and creativity. All of these stress external behaviors. He prefers to say "gifted behaviors" instead of gifted children and believes schools should enrich education for all students (Renzulli, 1994; Renzulli & Reis, 1996). According to his research, it is their drive that singles gifted students out from others. DeLisle (2000) does not believe that giftedness is based solely on what a person does. He claims that giftedness is based on who a person is and not on whether he or she produces anything.

The idea of intelligence for educators has been greatly altered by Howard Gardner. He is opposed to one type of "general" intelligence. In his book, *Frames of Mind: The Theory of Multiple Intelligences* (1983), he proposes that there are many ways of being intelligent. The original book cited seven intelligences: linguistic, mathematical, kinesthetic, musical, interpersonal, intrapersonal, and spatial. Later, Gardner added the naturalistic intelligence and maintains now that he feels there are even more (Gardner, 2003). Instead of asking, "How intelligent are you?", this research has prompted educators to ask, "How are you intelligent?" Gardner's wife, Ellen Winner, who is a researcher at Boston College, believes that some people can be profoundly gifted in just one area. When this is the case, it might not be identified on an IQ test. She believes that giftedness is demonstrated when a person is especially precocious in one area, has a drive to master that area, and thinks in unusual ways in that area. Winner advocates that programs for gifted children include art and music in their definitions (Winner, 1996). Another well-known researcher named Barbara Clark explains that giftedness comes from the brain's ability to integrate functions in an accelerated manner. These gifted abilities are expressed through cognition, creativity, academics, leadership, visual arts, or performing arts (Clark, 1988).

Pulling All the Research Together

Throughout the most recent years, research has dramatically changed the manner of thinking about gifted individuals. No single child embodies every attribute described by researchers; however, educators and parents should be aware of the ways in which giftedness can be identified (ERIC Clearinghouse on Handicapped and Gifted Children, 1990). Today, most researchers in the field recognize that there are many ways of being gifted. Intelligence is not a single quality that affects students' abilities across every domain. For example, researchers agree that a particular student can be gifted in science, but not in math. Some might be talented in music, but not in writing. Most experts today agree that giftedness is shown when a child processes information and solves problems more quickly than others. Another reality is that a person's intelligence is not fossilized, but rather can change over time. As brains develop and students devote more time to learning, they might become gifted in a particular area. For example, one does not improve unless one spends time practicing or perfecting one's talent. A child will not produce great art unless he or she spends time painting and drawing to improve his/her talent. This can deeply impact educational pedagogy. Many teachers strive to strengthen all students' weaknesses in high-stakes tested areas, such as reading and math, by taking advantage of their strengths in other areas.

Why a Definition Matters

The definition of giftedness matters because school districts use it to identify their specific population of gifted students. The definition affects which assessments are chosen and which programs are created for servicing these students. The programs are often funded with categorical money, and educators are held accountable for the use of the funds.

The definition should encompass a broad range of giftedness. The programs planned for gifted children involve students from varying degrees of giftedness. Research shows that gifted children differ from each other as much as they differ from average children (Lovecky, 1992). Some will exceed the criteria set by established definitions, others will just meet the bottom line, and still there are a few that will not be identified because of the boundaries set by these definitions.

Problems can arise with the assessments chosen. The National Association for Gifted Children urges educators not to confuse the definition of giftedness with the instruments chosen to identify giftedness. They are merely to be used as a signal to determine if giftedness may be present (NAGC, 2005b). While an IQ score may be helpful in identifying many students, it can miss some highly gifted individuals. Not all students are good at taking tests, and some researchers have shown that there are cultural biases in IQ tests. Depending on the definition used, some special population students, like those who are poor, might be discriminated against. These students have not had the resources to allow for enrichment opportunities, and it will show in their knowledge base when compared to students who have had the exposure. Those who are physically challenged might experience discrimination as well. Research has shown that some definitions even discriminate against gender and race. These facts have influenced many districts into utilizing a variety of instruments when identifying gifted children in their districts.

Once a district has established a definition for giftedness, there is still the matter of which terms should be used—*gifted* or *talented*? Often, terms such as *genius*, *prodigy*, *superior*, and *exceptional* are applied to describe these students ("Giftedness and the Gifted," 1990). These terms can carry varying positive and negative connotations. Some like to use the terms gifted and talented interchangeably. Others use the term talented for people who are good in a particular field, but the word gifted is only reserved for a few who exceed far beyond the talented.

Definitions Used by the Federal Government, the States, and Districts

Most schools use various factors to identify gifted students. These include grades, achievement test scores, parent nominations, intelligence tests, teacher recommendations, self-nominations, and peer nominations. Sometimes school districts include these identification methods in their definitions. Take the time to investigate the official definition used by your state or district to identify gifted children. Examine what terms are used, which identification assessments are used, and what programs are available for students who qualify as gifted. Find out what steps a teacher can take when he or she believes that a student in the class may be gifted.

A starting point is to identify what the federal government uses in its definition. Many states may take their lead because of the funds involved in educational programs. The definition from the No Child Left Behind Act of 2001 states:

> The term "gifted and talented," when used with respect to students, children, or youth, means students, children, or youth who give evidence of high achievement capability in areas such as intellectual, creative, artistic, or leadership capacity, or in specific academic fields, and who need services or activities not ordinarily provided by the school in order to fully develop those capabilities. (Title IX, Part A, § 9101, No. 22)

Today, each state in the United States has a different definition for giftedness. The NAGC states in its definition that "[A] gifted person is someone who shows, or has the potential for showing, an exceptional level of performance in one or more areas of expression" (NAGC, 2005b, para. 4).

When writing a definition for giftedness, most school districts pay attention to the following categories. First, they set a cutoff point on the IQ scale. For example, a district might set a cutoff IQ score at 130. Students who score 130 (or above) are gifted in that district. They will be the students to receive gifted instruction in their schools. Second, each district decides how many students they will identify as gifted in proportion to their population. Many districts set their qualifications to identify only five percent of their student population as gifted based on a compilation of teacher, parent, and self nominations, grades, IQ tests, achievement tests, creativity tests, and product evaluations. Third, some use the word *talent* to identify the area (academically and aesthetically) in which students are gifted. Fourth, they include the term *creativity*; this category highlights students' creative products and shows how they have scored on creativity tests.

Common Misconceptions About Gifted Children

There are as many misconceptions about what to do with gifted children as there are definitions of what gifted means. As you examine the definitions of the term gifted, it becomes evident that gifted children have diverse educational needs as compared with the general population. The goal, then, is to find out how to meet those needs.

It is likely that you will hear the following in your conversations with others. Following each frequently heard comment is research-supported rationale to demonstrate why the misconceptions are inaccurate.

"Don't spend your time worrying about them. Gifted children are smart enough to get by without special services." On the contrary, research has proven that students need learning experiences appropriate for their abilities or else they will lose their motivation for learning. In order for the brain to maintain its level of development, students must be challenged (Clark, 1997).

"Aren't truly gifted students those who excel in every subject in school?" It is helpful to remember that gifted students are real people who have specific strengths and weaknesses. While there are a few who excel in almost all academic areas, there are also a few with learning disabilities (Winner, 1996).

"Gifted students are all the same. If you've met one, you've met them all." Gifted students are like any other group of students who have varied abilities and interests. No one has yet created a mold in which all gifted students fit. It is important to remember that not all gifted students will respond to the same teaching strategies, either (Parke, 1989).

According to NAGC (2005b), it is believed that approximately five percent of the total student population in the United States is considered gifted. This is about three million children. If a broader definition of giftedness is used, a school district could expect to identify up to 15 percent (Eric Clearinghouse on Handicapped and Gifted Children, 1990). This is a significant number of children who have special needs within the educational domain. It is a teacher's responsibility to search for the indicators of student potential and seek ways to nurture that ability further (Coleman, 2003). By effectively teaching gifted students, teachers can prepare them to fully realize their potential. This book will continue to explore how these students can best be served.

Additional Resources—Giftedness

Cochran, J. (1992). *What to do with the gifted child: Meeting the needs of the gifted child in the regular classroom.* Nashville, TN: Incentive Publications.

DeLisle, J. (2003). *The survival guide for teachers of gifted kids: How to plan, manage, and evaluate programs for gifted youth K–12.* Minneapolis, MN: Free Spirit Publishers.

Rogers, K. B. (2002). *Re-forming gifted education: How parents and teachers can match the program to the child.* Scottsdale, AZ: Great Potential Press.

Smutney, J. F. (1997). *Teaching young gifted children in the regular classroom: Identifying, nurturing, and challenging ages 4–9*. Minneapolis, MN: Free Spirit Publishers.

Strip, C. A. (2000). *Helping gifted children soar: A practical guide for parents and teachers*. Scottsdale, AZ: Great Potential Press.

Webb, J. T. (1989). *Guiding the gifted child: A practical source for parents and teachers*. Scottsdale, AZ: Great Potential Press.

Chapter 1 Reflection

1. What is the definition of giftedness according to your state or school district?

   _____

   _____

   _____

2. Why do you think it is important for districts to have their own definitions of giftedness?

   _____

   _____

   _____

3. Do you believe that your state or district definition leaves room for discrimination? Why or why not?

   _____

   _____

   _____

4. Do you believe that gifted students are being effectively identified in your school? Why or why not?

   _____

   _____

   _____

Who Are Gifted Learners?

Now that you have a definition for giftedness, this chapter will explore how to identify the wide variety of students who may qualify for gifted programs. They might be the straight A students who excel in all subjects and score high on the standardized tests given each year, but there are also gifted students who are underachievers and do not necessarily make good grades. Some straight A students simply have excellent study habits and are overachievers. In many schools, there are only provisions for gifted classes in language arts or math. Most of the time, it is a matter of finding the funding for gifted programs and the qualified teachers to teach these students, particularly in areas outside of language arts and math. Therefore, if students are gifted in areas such as the visual arts or music, most schools do not have the resources to advance these gifts. Giftedness is more than just developing skills more quickly or accomplishing the developmental milestones earlier; gifted children are "intensely curious, produce a constant stream of questions, learn quickly and remember easily, and think about the world differently than their age-mates" (Smutney, 2000, p. 2). The scenarios above might make you wonder how you can identify gifted children at all. Who is gifted? A teacher might just think that students with high test scores are the gifted ones. Chapter One mentioned that some gifted students do not test well, so these scores might be deceiving. It is also possible that these tests have too low of a ceiling for a gifted child. We might know that a gifted child is in the 99th percentile, but we don't know how much higher he or she could have scored. At times, the question of who is actually gifted can be tough to answer. This chapter will help teachers identify the gifted learners in their classes in order to provide the best education for all students.

The Difference Between Gifted and Bright Students

Are gifted children and bright children the same? This specific question presents a gray area. The issue is compounded by the accountability and funding issues tied to gifted programs. It is important that children are correctly placed into the school program that will most benefit them. In the review for eligibility, an educator has the following options: (1) to identify a student as needing the gifted program; (2) to declare the student eligible for review and assessment at a later date; or (3) to tentatively place a student and see whether the program is a good match for him/her (Coleman, 2003). Some researchers, like Joseph Renzulli, believe there is nothing wrong with including children who are bright, but perhaps not gifted in a gifted program, as long as they can keep up.

According to Renzulli, enrichment should be for all children (Renzulli & Reis, 1985; Renzulli, 1995).

To make things more complicated, some gifted students also have learning disabilities, which could overshadow their giftedness. In addition, some gifted students are English language learners, and a lower language acquisition level could make it difficult for them to score well on assessments only offered in English. These students tend to be underrepresented in gifted programs because of narrow definitions of intelligence, overreliance on standardized tests, and inadequate procedures for identification (Coleman, 2003).

Table 2.1 shows a comparison between a bright learner and a gifted learner. It is important to remember that the characteristics of all children can differ, and no one child will demonstrate all of the traits in a single column. However, the chart does give teachers a better idea of the differences between a bright student and a gifted student. When teachers know how to identify their gifted students, they can better support these gifted children with curriculum that will challenge their intellect.

Table 2.1: Characteristics of a Bright Child vs. a Gifted Child

The Bright Child	The Gifted Child
knows answers to questions	asks the questions that need to be answered
is interested in content	is curious about content
is attentive	is both mentally and physically involved
has good ideas	has unusual ideas
works very hard	doesn't need to work as hard as others, but has a good understanding
can answer the questions with hard work	likes to elaborately discuss the problem
is at the top of the class	is far beyond the top of the class
is interested in the debate	has strong opinions about the debate
learns easily	already knows the material
needs about eight repetitions to master topic	needs only one repetition to master topic
has a good understanding of ideas	creates the ideas and inferences
likes friends in his/her age group	likes the company of adults
completes assignments on time	initiates projects to do in class
is friendly and open	is intense and passionate
is good at copying ideas	creates the new ideas
is motivated by school	is motivated by learning
can absorb information	can manipulate information
is like a technician	is like an inventor
can memorize well	can guess well
likes order	likes complexity
is pleased with his/her successes	is critical of his/her successes

Chapter 1 also mentioned that gifted students can be gifted in various areas. Gifted students may be gifted in one single area or in a few. Characteristic charts can help to identify gifted children at a glance. Figure 2.1 shows the characteristics of various areas of giftedness distinguished by the National Association for Gifted Children (NAGC). It is important to recognize and nurture giftedness so that those who can do something about the skills can respond to them before the abilities diminish or become less recognizable (Smutney, 2000).

Figure 2.1: Characteristics of Various Areas of Giftedness

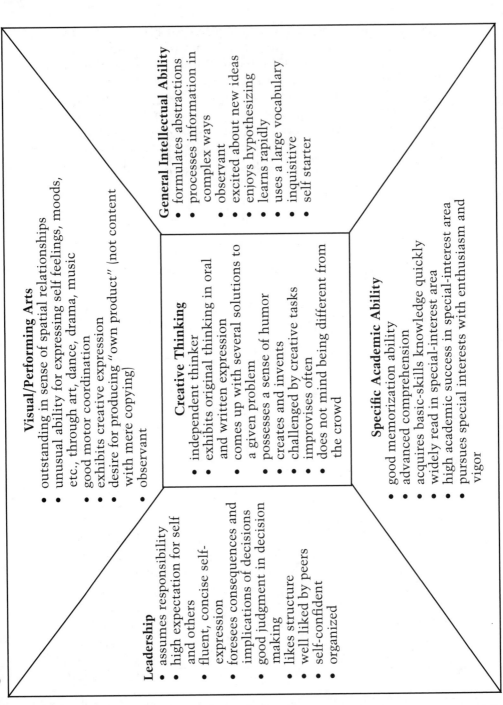

Visual/Performing Arts
- outstanding in sense of spatial relationships
- unusual ability for expressing self feelings, moods, etc., through art, dance, drama, music
- good motor coordination
- exhibits creative expression
- desire for producing "own product" (not content with mere copying)
- observant

General Intellectual Ability
- formulates abstractions
- processes information in complex ways
- observant
- excited about new ideas
- enjoys hypothesizing
- learns rapidly
- uses a large vocabulary
- inquisitive
- self starter

Creative Thinking
- independent thinker
- exhibits original thinking in oral and written expression
- comes up with several solutions to a given problem
- possesses a sense of humor
- creates and invents
- challenged by creative tasks
- improvises often
- does not mind being different from the crowd

Specific Academic Ability
- good memorization ability
- advanced comprehension
- acquires basic-skills knowledge quickly
- widely read in special-interest area
- high academic success in special-interest area
- pursues special interests with enthusiasm and vigor

Leadership
- assumes responsibility
- high expectation for self and others
- fluent, concise self-expression
- foresees consequences and implications of decisions
- good judgment in decision making
- likes structure
- well liked by peers
- self-confident
- organized

Source: Printed with permission from the National Association for Gifted Children (NAGC). Copyrighted material from NAGC, 1707 L Street, NW, Suite 550, Washington, DC 20036. This material may not be reproduced without permission from NAGC. For more information on NAGC and gifted children contact NAGC at (202) 785-4268 or visit their website at *http://www.nagc.org.*

Gifted Students Think Differently

In spite of the varied degrees of gifted characteristics, some are common among many of these students. One common characteristic explicitly stands out: Gifted students think differently! For example, here are some typical, mundane questions from a teacher who was trying to get her students to write about the sequence of events in everyday life:

1. What do you do just before you put on your shoes?
2. Right after you open your eyes what happens?
3. What do you do before you eat a candy bar?
4. Describe what happens when it is time to brush your teeth.

These questions seem rather straightforward. The answers seem obvious, but look how a highly gifted seven-year-old boy answers them with humor:

1. Just before I put on my shoes, I put on my lucky socks.
2. Right after I open my eyes, I go back to sleep.
3. Before I eat a candy bar, I admire it.
4. I hide the toothpaste, the toothbrush, and me.

Many times gifted students and their classmates don't see eye to eye. During a group project in second grade in which they had to create a desert model, John, a seven-year-old, got into an argument with his classmates because he wanted to put mountains in the model desert. Of course, mountains can be responsible for creating a desert. John was looking at the bigger picture, and his classmates did not understand this. Their intelligence can be amazing, too. John drew a very complex picture one day of a factory that incinerated completed homework (taken directly by a conveyer belt from the school) and made the ashes into souvenirs, which it sold back to the parents in a shop. His mother was not sure he was consciously aware of his irony, but she thought it was astute for a seven-year-old.

Gifted students may have the ability to accomplish tasks that they have never been explicitly taught. One mother recounted a day when her son Carter, who was five at the time, was provided wood, a hammer, nails, and glue. He asked his father to make the saw cuts because he was not allowed to use the saw, but otherwise, his parents just left him alone to do his project. After a while, Carter came in to get his two-year-old sister and announced that he had made her a bench where they could sit in the garden together. The father, who was a civil engineer, noticed that the bench was symmetrical and structurally sound for the two of them to sit on. The mother added that Carter could not tie his own shoe until after he turned seven and that he also had trouble following a series of instructions in large-group situations. Yet he had completed this bench project masterfully.

The gifted are often concerned with unusual topics that most children don't consider. David paced back and forth in his home looking very agitated. When his mother finally convinced him to tell her what was wrong, he blurted out his deep concerns over the idea of infinity saying, "Who thought of all the numbers and gave them names? I mean, if they go on to infinity, who could do that? How could they give all of them names before they died? Did they spend their whole life doing this and never finish?"

Susie had just turned six when she started taking piano lessons. This meant a trip into the city every week, and she very quickly figured out that the haggard-looking people she saw at intersections were down on their luck and homeless. It bothered her very much. So she thought of making up little bags of snacks for them. She put in apples, granola bars, cartons of orange juice, etc.

Her skeptical mother went along with the idea. They kept these in their car to hand out to them on Tuesdays when they went for her lesson. As she was finishing up assembling these bags she said, "Well, if they don't have much money, they probably can't buy vitamins, and you need vitamins to stay healthy." So she put vitamins in their snack bags. Her mother thought that Susie's idea was really going above and beyond the call of duty. She chuckled to herself about it, knowing that the people who received the snack bags probably wouldn't be expecting vitamins and might not know what to do with them. But her daughter was right, of course. People suffering from malnutrition are definitely in need of vitamins, so she didn't interfere with Susie's well-thought-out plan.

Gifted children are aware of their thinking, too. Chandler, a seven-year old, told his mother that he had been thinking about the length of peoples' lives. After giving his theory, he stated, "I still don't understand why people have to die. But I really think I'm right about this, I've been thinking about it a lot. But I don't know if other people think this, and I probably never will know because billions of people have already died and I can never ask them if they thought this or not." His mother had not heard him talk about this subject before that moment. She felt that most seven-year-olds don't think about these things, nor do they consider whether other people are thinking about these profound topics either.

Characteristics to Monitor

The situations in this chapter illustrate that it is a difficult task to categorize giftedness. One of the common identifying characteristics of gifted children is that they are so unique. Therefore, it is helpful to have a taxonomy or checklist of things to look for in your students. Remember, lists can help to identify, but they are by no means exhaustive, and not every gifted student will exhibit all the characteristics listed. The most effective method to distinguish and classify giftedness is to use a variety of methods over an extended time period. While the physical, social, and cognitive developmental aspects tend to be rapid and variable in children, the cognitive and motor skills characteristics can appear suddenly (Smutney, 2000). Thus, one single test at one single time would not accurately depict the giftedness of a student. Also, the term giftedness refers to a broad spectrum of abilities without being specific or dependent on one single measure or characteristic (NAGC, 2005b). The items presented in Table 2.2, adapted from Clark (1988), outline various categories of characteristics and identifying factors that may indicate that a student is gifted. It demonstrates a large range of behaviors that might be present across various types of traits. A teacher could use the list to inform and support a teacher recommendation for requesting that a student be assessed for a gifted student program.

Table 2.2: Categories of Characteristics of Gifted Students

Category	Characteristics
Cognitive	remember large amounts of information superior comprehension interested in many things highly curious advanced language and verbal development unusually large capacity for processing information able to think quickly and with flexibility have many ideas spend extended amounts of time on projects make unusual connections generate many original ideas and unique solutions integrate ideas and disciplines use and form conceptual frameworks early on evaluate approach toward self and others have a remarkable intensity driven by goals
Physical	heightened sensory awareness unusual discrepancy between physical and intellectual development low tolerance for lag between their standards and their athletic skills
Affective	large accumulation of information about emotions unusual sensitivity to the feelings of others sense of humor heightened self-awareness, feelings of being different idealistic and sense of justice inner locus of control unusual emotional depth and intensity high expectations of self/others are perfectionists need consistency between values/actions high levels of moral judgment
Intuitive	early involvement and concern for intuitive knowing open to intuitive experiences creativity apparent in all areas of endeavor ability to predict interest in future
Societal	strongly motivated by self actualization needs advanced capacity for conceptualizing and solving societal problems possess leadership qualities involvement with the meta-needs of society (justice, truth, beauty)

Source: Adapted with permission from *Growing Up Gifted: Developing the Potential of Children at Home and at School* (3rd ed.), by Barbara Clark. Copyright © 1988 by Prentice Hall Publishing.

When Giftedness Causes Problems

When teachers are not prepared or aware, gifted traits can seem to cause problems in the classroom. Because gifted children tend to be overly sensitive to social cues and overly critical of themselves and others, their peer relationships may suffer as they are often actively involved in non-social academic behaviors and bored with the culture of their age group (Hoge & Renzulli, 1991). Some young students have a large vocabulary and often seem more mature than their peers. This can cause teachers to expect more of these students than what they can deliver. The need that gifted students have to question everything can leave teachers feeling threatened and disrespected. Teachers will find that it is not easy to hide their lack of knowledge from gifted students. They must be secure enough to admit they don't know everything. Gifted students are intuitive and seldom need systematic instructions. However, teachers must not forget that they still need content instruction and assistance, especially in high-challenge tasks that need teacher support for a higher risk of effort (Tomlinson, 1997). They often have trouble with classroom transitions and moving on to the next topic or activity because they are so focused on what they are doing. They also have a wide array of interests, which can result in projects being left unfinished. Some are so consumed with perfection, that they are unwilling to try new things for fear of failure. Their creativity can be misconceived as being nonconforming and rebellious. Many gifted students find it hard to work with others, and they become impatient with those who cannot grasp the material quickly. This can severely disrupt cooperative groups and leave gifted students isolated and unsocial.

Teachers can ward off these problems by being aware of them before they begin. Gifted students need teachers who can respond to them with sensitivity, understanding, and patience. They need teachers who are flexible and open to new ideas, as well as teachers who respect imagination and creativity. By providing a safe environment for students, teachers can watch these gifted students bloom and flourish academically and socially.

Additional Resources—Gifted Characteristics

Ford, D. (2005). *Teaching culturally diverse gifted students.* Waco, TX: Prufrock Press.

Friedrichs, T. (2005). *Distinguishing characteristics of gifted students with disabilities.* Waco, TX: Prufrock Press.

Johnsen, S. (2005). *Identifying gifted students: A step-by-step guide.* Waco, TX: Prufrock Press.

Matthews, M. (2005). *Gifted English language learners.* Waco, TX: Prufrock Press.

Chapter 2 Reflection

1. How would you describe gifted students in your classroom (or identify students that you might recommend for gifted programs in the future)? Use Table 2.1 and Figure 2.1 to help you describe them.

_____

_____

_____

2. How are the gifted students in your classroom similar to one another?

_____

_____

_____

3. How are the gifted students in your classroom different from one another?

_____

_____

_____

4. Describe some of the problems that teachers with gifted students have complained about at your school. What advice would you give to a colleague who was sharing these problems with you?

_____

_____

_____

Creating a Differentiated Classroom for Gifted Students

It is the middle of summer and you have heard something awful. Rumor has it that your district has done away with its gifted pull-out program. Instead, each classroom teacher will be required to differentiate curriculum for these gifted learners. You may be in a district that has always had classrooms with full inclusion of gifted students and you have just found out that you will have gifted students in your classroom. Phrases like *heterogeneous classrooms, scaffolding,* and *content, process,* and *product* are likely to swirl in your mind. One reason this situation might be so worrisome is that teachers are under a lot of pressure to teach the appropriate content standards so that *all* students can demonstrate mastery. Continuous academic progress for all students is a goal that all teachers have, yet what does this mean for the gifted student who can easily demonstrate mastery of the content already? When a teacher is presented with such a wide array of student ability, the pressure becomes increasingly challenging. Many teachers know that differentiation is important, but they may not fully be able to explain how they plan to differentiate instruction for the various ability levels in their classrooms. Teachers often feel comfortable modifying curriculum to meet the needs of struggling students but not quite as comfortable making similar adjustments for gifted students (Winebrenner, 1992). However, if a classroom is truly differentiated, this means that *each* child's needs are met by the curriculum and strategies, regardless of high or low ability. To combat these common reservations, this chapter will explore the topic of differentiation and how a teacher can effectively integrate differentiated practices into a classroom that includes gifted students.

What Is Differentiation?

Differentiation is a popular word in education today. Educators speak of differentiated curriculum, differentiated instruction, differentiated practices, and differentiated assessment. However, individual teachers may struggle to actually clearly define what a differentiated classroom looks like. According to Tomlinson (1995), "A differentiated classroom offers a variety of learning options designed to tap into different readiness levels, interests, and learning profiles" (p. 1). This means that a differentiated classroom must address the varied needs of the wide range of students in a single classroom. "Using differentiation in the classroom means designing and implementing curriculum, teaching strategies, and assessments to meet the needs, interests, and abilities of all students" (Kirchner & Inman, 2005, p. 10). The need for differentiation pertains to students with special needs, students who are English Language Learners, and as it applies in this book, gifted students. In their official position paper on the subject, the National Association for Gifted Children notes that differentiation for gifted students includes "acceleration of instruction, in-depth study, a high degree of complexity, advanced content, and/or variety in content and form" (NAGC, 1994).

In a differentiated classroom, students get to explore subject matter in different ways. As national and state standards drive the content in the classroom, differentiation becomes necessary if students have already mastered the grade-level appropriate content. These students need credit for their mastery in addition to the opportunity to explore that same content vertically with in-depth exploration beyond the particular grade-level expectations (Inman & Roberts, 2006). Perhaps the teacher provides different process activities for learning the content. Perhaps the teacher grants varied opportunities for demonstrating what they have learned. The activities and end products are sense-making and appropriate to the students' individual levels. This helps the students understand the content. The students get a chance to show what they have learned in a variety of ways.

Characteristics in a Truly Differentiated Classroom

According to Tomlinson (2001), there are four characteristics that shape teaching and learning in a truly differentiated classroom. The first characteristic is that instruction is concept focused and principle driven. Everyone explores and applies key concepts, but the advanced learner has the opportunity to expand what he/she understands and apply it.

Secondly, differentiation builds in an on-going assessment of students' readiness as well as growth. Some students may surprise you and grow drastically over a month in their knowledge of various concepts. Teachers are to be continually assessing their students' needs so that they know how to guide, support, and move them ahead. Preassessment is an important aspect to this characteristic. Teachers find out which students already know the content before teaching the unit of study. One effective way to do this with gifted students is to present the five most difficult questions related to that unit, and if the gifted student knows four out of five of them, then he/she can move on to other material (Winebrenner, 1992). Preassessment is also important for gifted students because the process allows them to access their own prior knowledge on a subject so that they can creatively push themselves to higher levels and prepare their bright minds to learn what they need to in a new topic of study.

Thirdly, in a differentiated classroom, a teacher implements flexible grouping for his/her students. Students need opportunities to work independently, with partners, and in groups. Grouping is arranged according to the needs of the students and the purposes of the activity. This means that the grouping configurations could change throughout a single day of different learning activities. Grouping is flexible; students are not stuck in the same groups for the entire year for every learning activity. In a mixed-level classroom, the gifted students may be grouped together if they are working at a more advanced level of the same content on a particular project. Then, in another classroom activity, they might also be grouped heterogeneously by ability level and be given a cooperative task at a higher-thinking level of cognition but still working with their peers. The possibilities are as endless as the teacher is creative. Ineffective instruction for gifted learners includes cutting them off from affiliation with peers and teacher contact for long periods of time. Meaningful peer interaction is important for the learning process, social development, and emotional balance of gifted students (Tomlinson, 1997). When children work together in groups, they prepare for an essential life skill in the future work world. They also gain a sense of belonging, working together on similar but differentiated tasks (Winebrenner, 1992).

Finally, a differentiated classroom allows students to be active explorers. Instead of being a "sage on the stage," teachers become the "guide on the side." They are the facilitators who allow their students to be independent learners. In this role, teachers constantly check for understanding and monitor student activity so that they can continue to support student progress within the classroom. As a facilitator, the teacher can guide gifted students toward deeper understanding of the content at the same time as offering guidance to struggling students.

How Gifted Students Learn

Understanding how gifted students learn best is the indicator of how to differentiate curriculum to meet their needs. Teachers need to consider what motivates gifted students to want to learn. Think back on a time in your life when you completed a task that you thought was difficult. How did that make you feel when you completed it? Completing easy tasks does nothing for a person's self-confidence. Self-confidence only rises when we have the opportunity to complete a task that we first perceive as difficult.

Gifted children need these challenges to build their confidence. According to Susan Winebrenner, gifted students naturally identify themselves. She urges teachers to set up learning opportunities designed to motivate gifted students in the classroom. These types of learning opportunities magically draw out the students who need them (Winebrenner, 1992).

Many who have worked with gifted children know that they learn differently. This difference in learning is what poses the problems for most teachers. The goal of every good teacher is to teach his/her students. This statement implies that students will actually learn something that is being taught. It is critical that teachers consider how they will challenge these gifted students and how they can work to create a classroom that stimulates all students through differentiated lessons, open-ended activities, self-directed learning, and creativity. The first step in knowing how to do this is to understand how they learn.

Here is what is known about how gifted children learn:

1. Gifted children learn new information in shorter time frames and tend to remember what was taught better than the average student.

2. These exceptional children can observe concepts and ideas at more complex and abstract levels than most children their age.

3. At times, gifted children "learn" not to be so gifted when they quickly discover that being gifted only calls for additional work.

4. Gifted students have a passionate interest in selected topics and desire to spend large amounts of time on the topic before moving on to new material.

5. Gifted students need opportunities to express their own creativity so that it will grow and develop.

6. Like everyone else, gifted students have various ways through which they can demonstrate their intelligence.

According to the NAGC position paper on differentiation, there are various problems that can occur when teachers limit the learning experiences for gifted students: they may simply offer more of the same material or extra problems that are at the same level; they may not focus on the multiple levels of growth (i.e., cognitive, affective, physical, and intuitive); they may teach thinking skills in isolation from academic content; or they may give additional work that is not related to core curriculum at all (NAGC, 1994). These problems can be resolved by carefully planning differentiated instruction around the ways that gifted children learn. The section below looks at each aspect pertaining to how gifted students learn and then describes how teachers can offer the necessary differentiated instruction. Most of the recommended strategies are then detailed in the chapters that follow.

What Gifted Learners Need in School

1. ***Gifted children learn new information in shorter time frames and tend to remember what was taught better than the average student.*** If the class needs more time to learn a new concept, gifted students often become bored. Just imagine that you enrolled in a tap class at the local dance studio. You caught on quickly to the new steps the instructor demonstrates, but others in the class are struggling with the most basic steps. Rather than move on during the second lesson, the instructor decides to repeat the exact same lesson from the first class. This leaves you extremely bored and possibly angry. Do you stick it out knowing you are wasting your time? No, you drop the class and enroll in an advanced tap class that will teach you something new. Gifted students don't have the advantage of dropping their classes. Oftentimes they sit in their classes suffering through extreme boredom.

   Once a teacher understands that these students learn at a quicker pace, the teacher needs to create a plan to allow gifted students to learn something new. Curriculum compacting is one method teachers can use to meet the needs of gifted students. Differentiation for gifted students combines enrichment and acceleration strategies with flexibility and diversity (NAGC, 1994). Curriculum compacting, enrichment, and acceleration will be discussed further in Chapter 4.

2. ***These exceptional children can observe concepts and ideas at more complex and abstract levels than most children their age.*** To accommodate this, teachers can design lessons with more complex questions and activities. It is not effective to teach these higher-order thinking skills in isolation of the content (NAGC, 1994). The higher-order thinking skills should be infused in the content concepts with which gifted children are interacting. Process is another area where differentiation can benefit gifted learners. While some students are studying the solar system in order to remember and understand (a lower level of cognition), some students may be ready to apply, analyze, and synthesize information about the planets, while others yet may need to be evaluating in order to be involved in a learning process (Inman & Roberts, 2006). Two easy ways to differentiate by questioning and activities is to use Bloom's Taxonomy of Cognitive Thought or Sandra Kaplan's Differentiation by Depth and Complexity. Both of these questioning/activity techniques will be outlined in Chapters 5 and 6, respectively.

3. ***At times, gifted children "learn" not to be so gifted when they quickly discover that being gifted only calls for additional work.*** Designing lessons that differentiate by tiered assignments is one way to avoid giving gifted children (and others) busy work. Gifted students will not learn

appropriately in a challenging setting if they are simply given extra work at the same level that is already too easy for them. Tiered lessons don't provide more work for the gifted students; they just provide lessons that meet their ability levels as well as everyone else's in the classroom. Tiered assignments will be explained in Chapter 7.

4. ***Gifted students have a passionate interest in selected topics and desire to spend large amounts of time on the topic before moving on to new material.*** Gifted students may resent a fast-paced moving classroom that takes no notice of their inquisitiveness on a topic before moving on to new material. Teachers can meet this need by using individualized learning contracts. Chapter 8 will cover learning contracts in detail.

5. ***Gifted students need opportunities to express their own creativity so that it will grow and develop.*** Teaching students how to solve problems creatively will help them to be problem solvers in real life. If there is something exciting in the news that is a problem for your community, set up lessons that involve your students. Some teachers have had their students tackle pollution of a local lake, problems with finding permanent homes for pets from the humane society, or raising community awareness of local charities. Gifted students should also be given the opportunity to demonstrate what they have learned in a manner that matches their creativity. "Differentiation occurs when you encourage your students to demonstrate their learning in products that match them: their learning style, their interests, their multiple intelligences. And the assessment of those projects holds all children to high standards" (Inman & Roberts, 2006). Methods of creative problem solving will be discussed in Chapter 9.

6. ***Like everyone else, gifted students have various ways through which they can demonstrate their intelligence.*** Teachers can search for ways to allow gifted students to express themselves in different ways by differentiating curriculum along various areas of interest. These choices can make great open-ended activities that accommodate students' learning styles and allow individual creativity to bloom. Creating curriculum choices modeled after the theory of Multiple Intelligences is one way teachers can meet the different learning styles in the classroom. Multiple Intelligences will be covered in Chapter 10.

Additional Resources—Creating a Classroom for Gifted Students

Kaplan, S. N. (2002). *Curriculum starter cards: Developing differentiated lessons for gifted students.* Waco, TX: Prufrock Press.

Reis, S. M. (2003). *Curriculum for gifted and talented students.* Thousand Oaks, CA: Corwin Press.

Tomlinson, C. A. (2004). *Differentiation for gifted and talented students.* Thousand Oaks, CA: Corwin Press.

Chapter 3 Reflection

1. What are some of the ways your classroom instruction has already been differentiated?

   _____

   _____

   _____

   _____

   _____

2. What characteristics of a differentiated classroom would you like to improve upon or add in the near future?

   _____

   _____

   _____

   _____

   _____

3. Why do gifted students in your classroom need differentiation?

   _____

   _____

   _____

   _____

   _____

Curriculum Compacting

As this book continues to address effective practices of differentiation for gifted students, consider the following hypothetical student. There is a student who is highly motivated and consistently finishes assignments early. Work is always properly completed, and it appears that this student knows the topic very well. The student occasionally expresses an interest in pursuing other topics instead of the topics listed on your planner. The student seems bored and often creates games and puzzles in class. These characteristics make this student a prime candidate for curriculum compacting.

Curriculum compacting is a differentiation strategy that creates a challenging learning environment for gifted students. It also guarantees that these students know the basic curriculum. It is inappropriate to expect gifted students to do what they already know how to do and then have to wait for others to learn. It is also not suitable to have them simply do more of the same work just because they can get through it faster (Tomlinson, 1997). With curriculum compacting, students finally get the opportunity to participate in meaningful activities in an accelerated or enriching atmosphere. Grade-level textbooks are often too simple for gifted students, and they include a lot of repetition and review (Reis et al., 1993). Curriculum compacting allows students to test out of what they already know. In effect, their advanced knowledge allows them to "buy time" for other fast-paced accelerated activities or in-depth enrichment activities.

How do teachers know when their students need curriculum compacting? If students consistently finish assignments more quickly than others in the class, seem bored during classroom instruction, and ask questions that demonstrate familiarity with concepts being taught, they probably need the curriculum compacted. Curriculum compacting is a technique that has been field-tested for students identified as gifted, yet is also thought to be an effective way to modify curriculum for all students who demonstrate high ability (Reis et al., 1993). At times, classroom performance does not always show whether these students can do more. Some classroom underachievers will test very high but often perform at average or below-average levels in class. This happens because they are bored or they equate being smart with having to complete more work. Curriculum compacting can make all the difference in their classroom performance.

Renzulli and Reis' Research on Curriculum Compacting

Much of the research concerning curriculum compacting is attributed to Joseph Renzulli and Sally Reis. Reis and Renzulli (1992) say that the goals of curriculum compacting are to allow for students to do work at a pace that is equal to their ability, to create a learning environment that is challenging, to guarantee that students have a proficient knowledge of basic curriculum, and to provide time for accelerated and enriching activities.

They have outlined three basic needs of gifted students in the regular classroom. First, they say that gifted students need regular opportunities to show what they know. Secondly, these students need to receive credit for what they already know. Finally, gifted students need to spend their classroom time on enriching and accelerated activities that challenge them (Reis, Burns, & Renzulli, 1992).

Table 4.1 shows the seven basic steps for curriculum compacting that teachers should consider when compacting the curriculum (Reis, Burns, & Renzulli, 1992).

Table 4.1: Basic Steps for Curriculum Compacting

1. Establish the goals and outcomes of any given unit.
2. Create a pretest for students on what they know in relation to these objectives.
3. Identify students who might be candidates for curriculum compacting.
4. Administer the pretest to selected students.
5. For those students who show high levels of mastery on the pretest, modify any part of the curriculum that is not mastered to allow it to be completed at a faster pace than the rest of the class.
6. Once the selected students have completed the modified lessons, provide a list of alternative enriching or accelerated activities from which these students may choose.
7. Document their proficiencies and keep detailed records of these instructional options available to each student. You can use these for reporting to parents and also to inform next year's teachers of each student's progress.

How to Begin Compacting the Curriculum

The first time you compact the curriculum, it is important to remember to start small. Begin with just one standards-based unit of study in a content area. Create a pretest that includes what students need to know about this subject. Choose two or three students who have mastered the objectives. Then plan alternative activities for these students to complete. As you become more familiar with compacting the curriculum, you can add different content areas and modify the curriculum for more students. Some teachers find that it is best to offer all students the option to take the pretest. Not all will want to take the pretest, but no one can complain when students who have mastered the curriculum are doing different work. In effect, you have given the same opportunity to all students if they choose to take the pretest. Joseph Renzulli and Linda Smith created a widely-used form that documents which compacting services are provided to students. It is called "The Compactor" (Renzulli & Smith, 1978). The chart format is divided into three columns where the teacher sequentially plans and records which curriculum areas need to be compacted with evidence (such as pretests), which procedures to use to guarantee mastery of grade-level objectives, and finally which specific acceleration and/or enrichment activities will advance the learning process for the student. This book uses adapted curriculum compacting forms to show examples where enrichment and acceleration were provided. Look on pages 57 and 58 at Figures 4.1 and 4.2 for these examples. At the end of this chapter, page 59 provides a blank sample compacting form that is provided for your curriculum planning.

Should I Use Enrichment or Acceleration?

The final component of curriculum compacting involves choosing specific strategies for the process of content advancement. Specifically, a teacher can choose to enrich the content or to accelerate the content. Whichever strategy is chosen, these activities should reflect an appropriate challenge and rigor that matches the students' abilities and interests (Reis et al., 1993). Enrichment activities provide a greater depth and breadth to learning. The content is usually self-selected by individual students and more complex in nature. Students can create original or creative products. Accelerated activities offer students the option of advancing through the curriculum at a fast pace. "Enrichment strategies might include: self-selected independent investigations, mini-courses, advanced content, mentorships, and alternative reading assignments. Acceleration might include the use of material from the next unit or chapter, the use of chronological grade level textbooks or the completion of advanced work with a tutor or mentor" (Reis et al., 1993, p. 27). Curriculum should match the ability level of each student regardless of grade level. For example, a third-grade student could be doing fifth-grade level math work.

The choice to use either enrichment or acceleration is dependent on the teacher and the individual school. Some schools can support acceleration and allow students to either advance to another grade level for a subject or provide the materials for acceleration within the class.

Whether or not to use enrichment or acceleration also depends on the students' needs. Many gifted students thrive on enrichment courses because it provides the opportunity to delve deeper into the curriculum.

Examples of Curriculum Compacting

On the following pages are examples of curriculum compacting forms for two students. A week before teaching the unit on the American Revolution, the teacher decides on her objectives and goals for the unit. Next, she tests her students to see who already knows the subject matter. One student, named Jeremy, already knows a lot about the American Revolution. He loves history and has read historical biographies since first grade. He also has a passion for writing and film making. Jeremy scores above 80% on the pretest. His teacher decides to compact the curriculum by omitting more than two-thirds of the content she was going to teach him. For the content that Jeremy does not already have, he joins the rest of the class for the lessons as usual. For the other two-thirds of the time, his teacher provides enriching activities that Jeremy will enjoy. These include preparing a documentary for either a radio program or a television program on any one person from the American Revolutionary time period. He also has the choice to write a storybook about one of these people and share it with a younger class. The teacher does not include an art activity because Jeremy does not like drawing, painting, or creating things with his hands. Figure 4.1 demonstrates how the teacher plans and records the enrichment opportunities that Jeremy is provided.

Figure 4.1: Sample Enrichment Curriculum Compacting Form

Student's Name	Subject/ Topic	How has the student shown mastery?	What other activities will be planned?	Choices for Compacting the Curriculum
Jeremy	American History: The American Revolution	He scored above 80% on the pretest	Jeremy will join the class on days they learn content he has not mastered.	1. Prepare a documentary on one person from the American Revolutionary time period using either audio or video equipment. 2. Write a storybook for a lower grade about the details of the American Revolution including causes and effects.

When approaching a unit on division, the teacher looks at her objectives and goals for the unit. She then creates a pretest for her students to see what they already know. Several students know how to divide and score above 80% on the pretest. For these students, she decides to accelerate the curriculum. The second example of compacting in Figure 4.2 shows accelerated activities. Emily already knows how to divide, so she is given accelerated lessons showing her how to perform long division. If the schedule with other grade levels can be worked out, Emily will join them for lessons on long division. Otherwise, her teacher will provide her with lessons on long division to be completed as an independent project and with other students in the class who are also having their curriculum accelerated. Emily, along with her classmates, works to prepare an introductory lesson to show the class how to solve problems using long division. Figure 4.2 demonstrates how the teacher documents the acceleration opportunities that Emily is provided.

Figure 4.2: Sample Acceleration Curriculum Compacting Form

Student's Name	Subject/ Topic	How has the student shown mastery?	What other activities will be planned?	Choices for Compacting the Curriculum
Emily	Math (Division)	She scored a 90% on the pretest	Emily will work with the class on days they learn concepts she has not mastered.	1. Work on long division problems during the math hour. 2. Serve as a math consultant on one day and prepare a review lesson on long division for the class.

Page 59 provides a blank sample curriculum compacting form that teachers can use to plan and document enrichment and acceleration activities for gifted or high-ability students for which curriculum compacting is appropriate.

Additional Resources—Curriculum Compacting

Karnes, F. (2005). *Curriculum compacting: An easy start to differentiating for high potential students (Practical strategies series in gifted education)*. Waco, TX: Prufrock Press.

Starko, A. (1986). *It's about time: In-service strategies for curriculum compacting*. Mansfield Center, CT: Creative Learning Press.

Curriculum Compacting Form

Student's name	Subject/Topic	How has the student shown mastery?	What other activities will be planned?	Choices for Compacting the Curriculum

Chapter 4 Reflection

1. How can you find out which students already know the material that you will be covering in the next unit? Be specific about what you will do.

   _____

   _____

   _____

   _____

   _____

2. Consider the process of curriculum compacting. Write some examples of how you might try to compact the curriculum in your classroom.

   _____

   _____

   _____

   _____

   _____

3. What are some ways you could organize and manage alternative activities for these students?

   _____

   _____

   _____

   _____

   _____

Questioning
Techniques

If you had the chance to walk into a variety of different classrooms today, one striking similarity you might find is that the teachers are doing most of the talking and asking the majority of the questions. In one study, teachers in an elementary school reported that they thought they were asking about 12 to 20 questions every 30 minutes. However, the study showed that every half hour these elementary school teachers asked from 45 to 150 questions. (Fillippone, 1998). Other studies say that teachers are spending up to 80% of the school day asking questions (Brualdi, 2001). This situation leaves very little time for students to ask questions. Think about the characteristics of gifted children that were listed in Chapter Two. Gifted students are highly curious and need to ask questions. They are not content with merely answering the questions, especially if these questions require very little thinking on their part.

Various studies have also examined what kinds of questions teachers ask during a typical lesson. Most questions presented in the classroom are the types of questions that require very little thinking (Fillippone, 1998; Mueller, 1972); for example: *Who is the main character in this story? When did the American Revolution begin? What is the answer to this math problem?* Other frequent questions posed by teachers require no more than a "yes" or "no" response. This is not to say that lower-levels of recalling and remembering information have no place within a lesson. Questions that ask *what*, *when*, *who*, and questions that require "yes" and "no" responses can be a quick way for teachers to check for understanding before moving on. In fact, studies show that a combination of higher- and lower-cognitive questions is more effective than the exclusion of one or the other (Cotton, 1988). Yet, these types of questions often leave gifted learners (as well as many of the other students in the classroom) frustrated and bored. Simple questions such as these do not challenge most students to think, especially gifted students. When students are not thinking or engaging their minds, they are not learning. This happens when teachers do not know how to ask good questions. As a result, students do not know how to ask good questions either.

Why Do Teachers Use Questioning?

Teachers use the strategy of questioning in a classroom for a variety of reasons. Questions can keep students actively engaged in a lesson, students can express ideas and hear different explanations offered by peers, teachers check for understanding through a lesson with questions, and teachers can use them to reevaluate the pace and direction of a lesson (Brualdi, 2001). In fact, researchers have found that instruction is more effective when questions are being asked (Cotton, 1988). However, even with these good intentions, teachers may underestimate the value that the right kind of questions has on a student's learning process. All students need to know how to ask good questions that require thinking. When students learn how to ask good questions, they can apply it to their own learning as a strategy for comprehending new content at deeper levels. Teachers support students in becoming strategic when they explicitly teach them how to determine what levels of questions they are asked (Cotton, 1988). As students learn to answer different levels of questions, they learn to ask these same levels of questions when they approach new content. Teachers cannot inspire their students to be good question askers unless the teachers first learn how to ask good questions themselves. Then, they need to model and teach the correct way to ask the types of questions that make students think. Finally, they need to provide the students with ample opportunities to practice and use good questions in order to further inspire their individual learning.

What Makes a Good Question?

Questions should stimulate further thought, motivate action, or excite the learner with possibilities. When it comes to inspiring gifted learners toward these goals, not all questions are good questions. Good questions should make these learners think, pause, and reflect, rather than race to answer them. Good questions don't always have one right answer. Not only do they foster interaction between teacher and students, good questions require students to think beyond the factual knowledge and use knowledge to problem solve, analyze, and evaluate (Brualdi, 2001).

Gifted students are naturals at asking good questions because they are often curious about the next level beyond the basic concept. The questions they think about are complex, ambiguous, and sometimes hard to answer. These questions stem from their desire to learn and make the lessons meaningful. This process of learning to ask good questions is beneficial for all students, but it is essential in the instruction of gifted students. They need questions that will challenge them to actively explore and discover (Berger, 1991). Some questions, such as considering possibilities in "what if" questions, stimulate new and unconventional ways for gifted students to explore a new subject and encourage creative thinking (Smutney, 2000).

Most educators agree that they want to help their students become great thinkers. Great thinkers must begin by learning how to ask great questions. Not all forms of thinking are the same. Thinking occurs at various degrees depending on the depth of the questions. When teachers ask higher-level questions, they will produce deeper levels of learning (Hamaker, 1986; Pressley et al., 1992).

How Can Teachers Ask Good Questions?

Good questions require higher-level thinking (Brualdi, 2001). However, there is also a need for questions at higher levels to take the learning process a step further for students. In order to use higher levels of thinking, a good question should begin with any of these words: *why, how,* and *which.*

When a question begins with *why,* students scrutinize cause-and-effect relationships. *Why* questions require the asker and the responder to consider aim, intention, and reasoning. Young inquisitive children naturally ask questions that begin with the word *why.* Gifted learners will use these questions for figuring out the reasons beyond simple answers. *Why is the sky blue? Why do I get goose bumps? Why do dogs bark?*

Questions that begin with *how* aid in problem-solving situations. It is a form of synthesizing information. This category of questions will help gifted students in their desire to change and improve. Inventors often ask the *how* questions that spurn new inventions. This type of question can also improve businesses and repair items. *How will I earn money this summer? How will the dwarves defeat the dragon? How can I get more advertising for the school newspaper?*

Questions that begin with *which* are decision-making questions. They require one to compare evidence or clearly-stated criteria in the process of making choices. *Which* questions can help gifted students determine their paths and make decisions. *Which neighborhood is best to live in? Which career path should I pursue? Which college is best?*

In a classroom that celebrates the discovery of content, the teacher models these forms of effective questions, teaches the students how to use them while exploring subject matter, and most importantly, allows the students the time and practice opportunities to learn how to ask them, too. There are numerous models of questioning, but this chapter will explore how Bloom's Taxonomy of the Cognitive Domain can support teachers in using the right kinds of questions.

Bloom's Taxonomy of Cognitive Thought

Benjamin Bloom, along with a group of educational psychologists, proposed a plan to classify levels of cognitive thinking. The plan emerged in the book *Taxonomy of Educational Objectives, Handbook I: The Cognitive Domain* (Bloom, Englehart, Furst, Hill, & Krathwohl, 1956) with what has become popularly known as Bloom's Taxonomy. Bloom's "research and writing guided the development of innumerable educational programs and provided powerful new insights into the untapped potential of educators to have all students learn well" (Guskey, 2001, p. 1).

In the last five decades, educators have adopted Bloom's Taxonomy as a hierarchy of questions that progress from less to more complex levels of cognition. The succession of increasing cognitive skills allows teachers to identify the level at which students are thinking. It also provides a framework for modifying the process of learning for gifted students (Berger, 1991).

Many teachers see this taxonomy like a ladder or pyramid, working from the bottom with knowledge questions and moving up to the evaluative questions. However, for gifted students, teachers need to make sure to ask the appropriate questions for them, instead of moving along the ladder of cognition each time. Questions that have students analyzing, synthesizing, and evaluating are more appropriate for gifted learners. These kinds of questions help gifted learners connect what they are learning to the bigger world (Berger, 1991). As an example, students can be challenged to figure out why test scores are low in a particular district. This type of question requires students to acquire, analyze, and synthesize information in order to arrive at a likely answer and then move on to initiating a working solution.

Bloom's Taxonomy is a useful model for differentiating the curriculum easily. Teachers are providing group interaction, flexible pacing of lessons, and guidance through self-management of tasks in gifted classrooms where the differentiation of questioning and thinking is in place (Berger, 1991). Students who need the background information can complete the knowledge and comprehension questions and activities. Students who need to use the information they know, can do the application or synthesis activities and questions. Finally, the gifted children can work on activities that involve synthesis and evaluation.

In the progression toward the more advanced levels of thinking, students analyze by breaking things into smaller parts, synthesize when they think creatively, and evaluate when they make substantiated judgments. This description is easily applied to gifted students. Most gifted students will find the lower-level questions, including knowledge, comprehension, and application questions, easy to respond to. Therefore, it is important to offer them the more difficult, challenging questions that cause them to think. Otherwise, they might become bored, answering only questions that they already know and don't have to really think about.

The rest of this chapter will discuss the task words commonly associated with each level of Bloom's Taxonomy. Teachers use these task words to assign classroom activities. The task words are also easily adapted into questions that challenge students to formulate various levels of responses.

Figure 5.1 on page 68 shows the levels of Bloom's Taxonomy. For background information, all of the levels of questioning are included in the figure, although the book will be focusing on the three highest levels of cognition as they relate to the education of gifted students in the pages that follow.

Figure 5.1: Bloom's Taxonomy

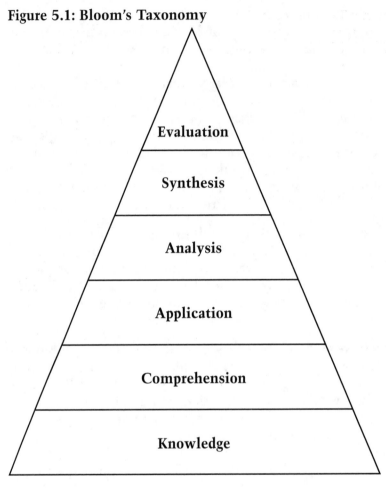

Table 5.1 on page 69 shows the task words associated with each level of Bloom's Taxonomy. Teachers differentiate their instruction by assigning a certain task (or formulating a question using a task word) that directs students to think along a certain level of cognition. These task words are excellent to include when planning learning objectives. All students can be moved along various levels of cognition within any given lesson. When designing questions and activities for gifted students, generally teachers should aim for activities that prompt analysis, synthesis, and evaluation.

Table 5.1: Bloom's Taxonomy Progression of Student Task Words

Knowledge skills require that students . . .	Comprehension skills require that students . . .	Application skills require that students . . .
tell	restate	demonstrate
recite	give examples	build
list	explain	cook
memorize	summarize	compute
remember	translate	produce
define	show symbols	discover
locate	edit	choose
describe	distinguish	apply
identify	estimate	dramatize
name	predict	employ
match	generalize	illustrate
arrange	classify	operate
duplicate	describe	practice
label	discuss	schedule
order	express	sketch
recognize	indicate	solve
relate	locate	use
recall	recognize	write
repeat	report	use guides, maps, charts, etc.
reproduce	restate	
state	review	
	select	

Analysis questions require that students . . .	Synthesis questions require that students . . .	Evaluation questions require that students . . .
investigate	forecast	judge
classify	imagine	evaluate
examine	categorize	give opinions
categorize	develop	recommend
compare	formulate	prioritize
contrast	manage	prove
solve	compose	critique
diagram	design	appraise
differentiate	invent	compare
test for	organize	conclude
outline	prepare	justify
distinguish	propose	criticize
	create	interpret
	hypothesize	argue
	construct	assess
	combine	defend
	compile	estimate
	reconstruct	predict
	summarize	rate
	plan	support
	write	value
	arrange	
	assemble	
	collect	
	rearrange parts	
	set up	

Effective Use of the Higher Levels of Thinking for Gifted Students

As gifted students require challenging material to further push their learning process, teachers can use the task words to encourage the use of Analysis, Synthesis, and Evaluation. These will inspire gifted students to actively practice the higher levels of cognition in their daily classroom tasks. When gifted students use **Analysis** skills, they examine relationships between parts of information as they seek to understand how the parts work all together. They look at the structure of a complicated topic of study and break it down into manageable parts. Part of Analysis is noting fallacies, as well. Questions using the analysis task words might prompt end-learning products, such as T-charts, mind maps, surveys, solutions, conclusions, and lists of attributes. Gifted students might be asked to compare the motives of two characters in history or to create a mind map that shows the parts of a good paragraph written at an advanced level. When gifted students use **Synthesis** skills, they generate new ideas by pulling different components of the information together. Synthesis requires the compilation of individual parts to make a new whole. Gifted students would need to organize a combination of information and arrange them in a way that makes sense. End products that demonstrate synthesis might be a new solution to a problem, an original hypothesis, creative stories, a new product, something that solves a problem, or experiments. Some specific examples of synthesis in the classroom are creating a new song that explains the jobs of a president and writing yourself as a new character into the story you are reading while revealing your motives for various actions. **Evaluation** skills require that gifted students provide proof in order to make judgments. They have to judge the value of something and explain the criteria used in support of their judgment. Evaluation products might be a grading rubric for the science fair, making judgments in a trial, writing a book review or an editorial, and completing a self assessment after a class project. Examples of evaluation include asking students to justify a controversial viewpoint taken on an event in history or to rate the effectiveness of a peer's proposal written to change the way something is done in a novel.

Sample Questions and Activities for the Classroom

In order to offer more guidance in how the teacher can help differentiate the curriculum for gifted students, the following examples provide questions using the task words, as well as task assignments that challenge students along higher levels of thinking. Bloom's Taxonomy can be used to create questions and activities that require higher-level thinking skills. While many of the specific task words are not present in the questions, their use is implied by the question itself. The level of thinking required by answering each question or responding to each activity task appears in parentheses.

Sample Questions from *The Bad Beginning* by Lemony Snicket

- Violet wishes she would have bought poison, but do you think she could have gone through with this idea? (Evaluation)
- How many eyes do you think are in Mr. Olaf's house? (Evaluation)
- What would you do if you had the beach all to yourself? (Evaluation)
- How would the story have changed if Violet had thrown the rock at Mr. Poe? (Synthesis)
- If you were Olaf, what top three things would you have the children do? (Synthesis)

- What is the difference between happiness and unhappiness? (Analysis)
- What kind of man would carve an image of an eye into his front door? (Analysis)
- Why did Justice Strauss help the children? Have you ever helped someone for those same reasons? (Analysis)

Sample Activities from *The Bad Beginning* by Lemony Snicket

- Imagine you can read Violet's thoughts. Make a list of ten original inventions that Violet has created in her mind. (Analysis)
- Mrs. Poe bought clothing for the Baudelaire children. Create a paper doll of one of the children. Then, using fabric, cut out one outfit from this awful new wardrobe and paste it on the paper doll. (Synthesis)
- Draw the Baudelaire family tree showing how Mr. Olaf is related to them. You will have to "invent" other family members to fill in the gaps. Be creative! (Analysis)
- Mr. Olaf's home is described in detail. Imagine this house could talk. What would it say to the Baudelaire children? Script this conversation. (Evaluation)
- Mr. Olaf obviously needs help decorating his house. The Baudelaire children have hired you to be his decorator. Design this first room on a sheet of paper showing what it would look like if you designed it using pictures from magazines, books, and newspapers. (Synthesis)
- Count Olaf has just given you a handful of rocks. Make at least two toys with these rocks. Turn in a picture of them along with an explanation of how to play with them. (Synthesis)

Sample Civil War Questions

- Do you agree with Lincoln's choice for Grant to be his new general? Why or why not? (Evaluation)
- If you were the president, what choice for general (besides Grant) would you have made? Show how this differs from what really happened. (Evaluation)
- What would happen if Gettysburg had happened first? Show how this switch would affect the other events in the Civil War. (Synthesis)
- Imagine that the South did not surrender. Describe how things would be different even today. (Synthesis)
- What are the four most important events from the Civil War? (Analysis)
- What were the three most important causes leading up to the Civil War? (Analysis)

Sample Economics Activities

- Compare two businesses. Compose a list contrasting the positives and negatives of these businesses. (Analysis)
- Develop a sample product that could be sold to teenagers. (Synthesis)
- Rate different advertisements that represent one common product. Justify why one advertisement is the best at selling that product. (Evaluation)
- Prioritize what you have to do in order to achieve your future career goals. (Evaluation)

Sample Science Energy Activities

- Assess how the people in your family conserve and waste energy. (Evaluation)
- Formulate a plan for conserving energy. (Synthesis)

- Investigate the sources of energy in your community. (Analysis)
- Compile energy-conserving tips to share with your classmates. (Synthesis)

Sample Math Cube Activity

Make a cube using the template in Figure 5.2. Fold in at each line and use tape to secure. Before taping, the following tasks (or similar ones) can be written on each face of the cube. The students can roll these cubes and complete the activities on the top of the cubes. Below are sample tasks for each face of the cube.

- Read a story problem. What other information do you need to solve this problem? (Analysis)
- Take three numbers. How many different kinds of problems can you create using these three numbers? (Analysis)
- Change one thing about the story problem. How does this change the answer? (Synthesis)
- Create a new problem for your class to solve. (Synthesis)
- Find a new way to solve a problem and defend it to a friend. (Evaluation)
- How well do you understand story problems? Create a chart that shows your answer. (Evaluation)

Figure 5.2: Sample Math Cube Template

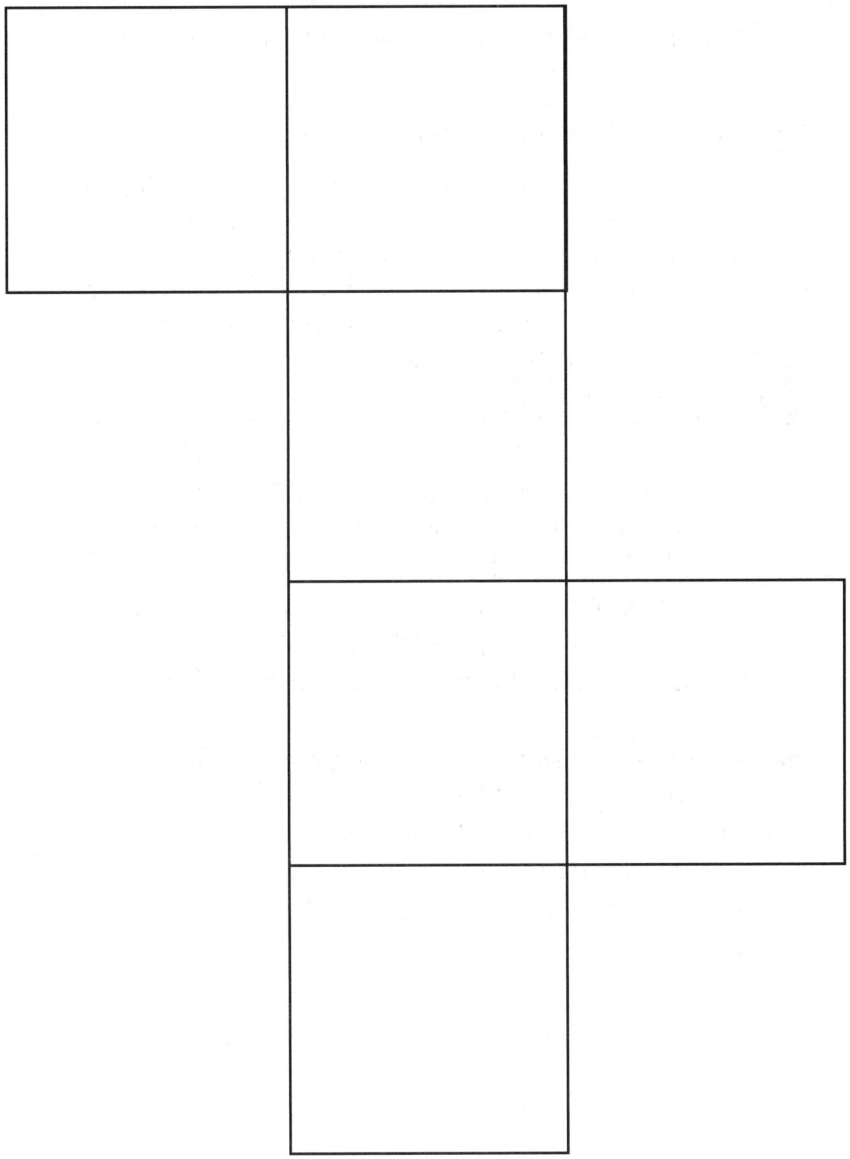

These activities highlight the possibilities for teachers as they begin to explore how they can apply the use of higher levels of thinking to the types of questions that they are asking in a classroom with gifted students. There is only so much instructional time in a school day. If questions are being asked by teachers or by students, it is vital that they are good questions that inspire further exploration of the content. Furthermore, teachers can utilize the various task words associated with each level of cognition to really inspire gifted students to extend their already brilliant minds.

Additional Resources—Bloom's Taxonomy

Anderson, L. (2000). *A taxonomy for learning, teaching, and assessing: A revision of Bloom's taxonomy of educational objectives*. Upper Saddle River, NJ: Longman Publishing.

Marzano, R. (2000). *Designing a new taxonomy of educational objectives*. Thousand Oaks, CA: Corwin Press.

Shaunessy, E. (2005). *Questioning strategies for teaching the gifted*. Waco, TX: Prufrock Press.

Chapter 5 Reflection

1. Reflect on your use of questions in the classroom. Describe what types of questions you use and why you use questioning techniques.

   _____

   _____

   _____

2. How do you think you can model good questioning techniques to students?

   _____

   _____

   _____

3. What do you think is the connection between good questions and the task words associated with Bloom's Taxonomy?

   _____

   _____

   _____

4. Describe the types of questions you use with your gifted students. Practice writing sample questions that inspire higher-level thinking.

   _____

   _____

   _____

Differentiation by Depth and Complexity

The idea of differentiating questions by depth and complexity is attributed to Sandra Kaplan. She sees both depth and complexity as interrelated, reinforcing each other. By differentiating the curriculum using depth and complexity, curricular expectations are defined clearly and students stay more focused, asking questions to increase their knowledge. Sandra Kaplan, an associate clinical professor for learning and instruction at the University of Southern California, believes that teachers should move their gifted students toward more depth and complexity. She describes eight strategies teachers can use to guide students to a greater depth of understanding and three strategies teachers can use to guide students through more complexity. These strategies not only raise the ceiling for gifted students, they help all students to advance their thinking abilities (Kaplan, 2005).

Sandra Kaplan's Dimensions of Depth

What does it mean to move students toward more depth in the curriculum? When students experience the curriculum in depth, they explore it from concrete to abstract ideas, from familiar to unfamiliar concepts, and from known to unknown facts. Content is elaborated on and students engage in the investigation of new ideas and concepts. Students are encouraged to delve deeper into the content area and experience a more intense exploration of facts, generalizations, theories, concepts, and principals. To prompt students to investigate a topic, subject matter that includes patterns, trends, rules, unanswered questions, and ethical considerations is presented to them.

According to Kaplan, depth occurs when students understand the **language of a discipline**. This involves learning specialized vocabulary for particular disciplines. Teachers can ask how they can help their students learn the language that specialists use in this discipline. For example, what words do students need to know when studying warfare during the 1800s? A brief look at any book on the Civil War will reveal many words with which students are not familiar, and these words are important for students to fully understand the type of warfare used during the Civil War era.

Depth also occurs when students learn the **details** of a discipline. Details refer to the parts and variables. Teachers can prompt their students to ask about the parts, attributes, and variables of the discipline. The goal is to help students learn as many details about the topic as possible. For example, "What is important about Civil

War warfare?" One detail is that guns were not very accurate and sometimes bayonets were used because ammunition ran out.

Learning about **patterns** also provides depth for students. To understand patterns, students will look at repetition and predictability in a given topic. Teachers will encourage their students to look at the repetitions associated with the topic and review their reoccurrence over time. For example, "How has warfare stayed the same since the 1800s? "

When students study the **trends** associated with a discipline, they learn what influences that discipline. Trends refer to direction or action. To experience depth, teachers can have their students study all the factors that influence events. For example, "What determined where the battles were fought in the Civil War?"

Often while in a course of study, there are **unanswered questions** that students will come across while studying that discipline. At a first glance, there are times that students won't realize that there are unanswered questions. Challenging students to look for those unanswered questions in the content is a way to add depth to curriculum. For example, "Why did General Robert E. Lee give General Pickett orders to charge the hillside?"

Every discipline has **rules** that govern it and form an unspoken hierarchy. Prompting students to look for those rules that bring order and structure adds depth to curriculum. For example, "What rules did men who served in the Confederate Army have to follow? Were there rules that the Union men had to follow?"

Many times, there are other dilemmas and controversial issues that relate to a discipline. Kaplan believes students should look at the **ethics** that relate to the topic, which include judging and forming opinions. For example, "How did men from the South who were against slavery defend their actions by fighting for the South? Is there a way to justify the South's desire to secede?"

Finally, the principles and generalizations also known as **big ideas** govern topics of study. Teachers should help their students look for those big ideas as they study and find out more about the topic. For example, "Overall, how did the Civil War impact the nation during the 1860s? How does it impact the nation today? What would life be like today if the Civil War had never taken place?"

Table 6.1 shows Kaplan's definitions along with icons that describe each of the eight categories of depth. Page 86 provides a blank sample planning sheet for differentiating by depth and complexity.

Table 6.1: Kaplan's Categories of Depth

	Category	Definition
	Language of the Disciplines	refers to learning the specialized and technological terms associated with a specific area of study or discipline
	Details	refer to the learning of the specific attributes, traits, and characteristics that describe a concept, theory, principle, and even a fact
	Patterns	refer to recurring events represented by details
	Trends	refer to the factors that influence events
	Unanswered Questions	refer to the ambiguities and gaps of information recognized within an area of discipline under study
	Rules	refer to the natural or person-made structure or order of things that explain the phenomena within an area of study
	Ethics	refer to the dilemmas or controversial issues that plague an area of study or discipline
	Big Ideas	refer to the generalizations, principles, and theories that distinguish themselves from the facts and concepts of the area or discipline under study

Sandra Kaplan's Dimensions of Complexity

Kaplan also believes that gifted students need curriculum that offers complexity. Complexity stresses the relationship between disciplines, how these relationships have changed over time, and how complexity uses a variety of perspectives when looking at issues. Complexity in content or subject matter exists in three main categories: over time, different perspectives, and interdisciplinary relationships.

Curriculum becomes more complex when students are challenged to look at relationships of a topic **over time**, from perspectives of the past, present, and future. Teachers can guide students to understand how to make connections and see interactions over a period of time. For example, "How will people view the causes surrounding the Civil War 100 years from now?"

There are **different perspectives** related to just about every topic. Having students analyze these differing points of view by looking at the multiple perspectives and opposing viewpoints can bring complexity to any curriculum. For example, teachers can have their students look at the Civil War from the viewpoints of soldiers, historians, and civilians. Teachers can also have students look at the difference between those siding with the Union and those siding with the Confederacy.

Adding complexity to the curriculum by having students examine **interdisciplinary relationships** refers to helping students find relationships across the disciplines. Teachers should guide their students to identify the cross-curricular connections in a topic. For example, teachers can ask: "How does patriotism cross disciplines? Are there songs, poems, and art related to this topic?"

Table 6.2 shows Kaplan's definitions accompanied by icons for each of the three categories of complexity. Page 86 provides a blank sample planning sheet for differentiating by depth and complexity.

Table 6.2: Kaplan's Categories of Complexity

	Category	Definition
	Over Time	refers to the understanding of time as an agent of change and recognition that the passage of time changes our knowledge of things
	Different Perspectives	refer to the concept that there are different viewpoints and that these perspectives alter the way ideas and objects are viewed and valued
	Interdisciplinary Relationships	refer to both integrated and interdisciplinary links in the curriculum; disciplinary connections can be made within, between, and among various areas of study or disciplines

Additional Resources—Depth and Complexity

Kaplan, S. (2002). *Curriculum starter cards: Developing differentiated lessons for gifted students.* Waco, TX: Prufrock Press.

Kaplan, S. (2002). *Lessons from the middle: High end learning for middle school students.* Waco, TX: Prufrock Press.

Roberts, J. (2005). *Practical strategies series: Enrichment opportunities for gifted learners.* Waco, TX: Prufrock Press.

My Planning Sheet for Differentiation by Depth and Complexity

	Category	Questions/Activities
	Language of the Disciplines	
	Details	
	Patterns	
	Trends	
	Unanswered Questions	
	Rules	
	Big Ideas	
	Ethics	
	Over Time	
	Different Perspectives	
	Interdisciplinary Relationships	

Chapter 6 Reflection

1. What does the term *depth* mean to you, and why do you think gifted children need it?

   _____

   _____

   _____

   _____

2. What are some ways you can add depth to your curriculum?

   _____

   _____

   _____

   _____

3. What does the term *complexity* mean to you, and why do you think gifted children need it?

   _____

   _____

   _____

   _____

4. What are some ways you can add complexity to your curriculum?

   _____

   _____

   _____

   _____

Tiered Assignments

> Even though students may learn in many ways, the essential skills and content they learn can remain steady. That is, students can take different roads to the same destination. (Tomlinson, 1999, p. 12)

What does Tomlinson mean when she says that students can take different roads to the same destination? This quote suggests that teachers do not have to fret about creating countless different lessons in order to reach all students. Students can all be taught the same lesson, but the activities throughout the lesson can be varied. One effective way to do this in a heterogeneous classroom is by implementing the idea of tiered assignments. Tiered instruction involves a teacher allowing different levels, or tiers, of activities, as students of varying levels of ability learn common content together in one classroom. This process is similar to the process known as scaffolding, in that teachers are providing the appropriate amount of support for students with varied needs and abilities while all students work toward the same content objectives.

By using tiered assignments, teachers take one topic and implement various activities based on different ability levels. This ensures that all students, regardless of ability, are expanding their knowledge. Even gifted students can use their own abilities to accomplish the particular tiered assignments set at their advanced levels. The essential ideas are the same for each lesson, but students explore them in varied ways. So, in effect, the students are taking different roads to the same destination.

Why Use Tiered Assignments?

Tiered instruction permits teachers to reorganize traditional educational practices that assume that all students have the same abilities and have the same backgrounds (Kingore, 2006). Often, students are given tasks that are too challenging, which may make them give up, or are too easy, which may make them bored. Each individual student comes to school with different readiness, interests, and learning profiles, so a "one-size-fits-all" model of instruction does not make sense for a teacher trying to cultivate continual growth (Tomlinson, 1995). With tiered assignments, the students are motivated to learn because they are given tasks that meet their ability levels, while taking into account their learning styles. Tiered assignments align the needs and abilities of students to the degree of instructional support that they will be offered by the teacher. It is also beneficial for teachers to push students just a little further than they are comfortable going, which leaves a level of satisfaction and importance. This builds self-esteem and motivation, because students are successful at completing the tasks.

In a classroom with gifted students, tiered instruction allows gifted students to receive instruction at a level for which they can pursue more knowledge than they already have. Author Bertie Kingore (2006) gives the metaphor of a stairwell in which students are working toward accessing a building of knowledge. The bottom step represents the tasks on which students with few skills will be working, and the top step represents the challenging level for gifted students. He maintains that there may not be students at each level; students move up through the various tiers of learning at different rates. Kingore also stresses that every tier needs modeling and support; even gifted students need direct instruction, interaction, direction, and feedback from the teacher.

How to Plan Tiered Lessons

In her book, *Differentiating Instruction in the Regular Classroom* (2001), author Diane Heacox offers the following three principles in organizing tiered lessons. First, teachers should be sure to introduce all activities with enthusiasm, regardless of the students' ability levels. All activities should be equally interesting and desirable. Second, teachers should be careful not to simply give more work for the advanced-level activities or less work for the basic-level activities. Finally, expect students to use key ideas, concepts, and/or skills.

Tomlinson adds that both sense-making activities and learning-end products can be tiered in a lesson (Tomlinson, 1995). Kingore (2006) reminds teachers that group membership in a particular tier needs to be flexible. The students should not always be stuck in the same levels, because their needs and abilities may change throughout the year. The teacher plans only the appropriate number of levels as needed in the classroom. This may vary by curricular area. Furthermore, the lowest tier in one classroom may be different than the lowest tier for another group of students, whether this pertains to the next year of students for an elementary school teacher or the next class period for a middle school or high school teacher. Finally, Kingore believes that all students in all tiers deserve the opportunity to be challenged and to work on higher-level thinking skills.

Table 7.1 shows some useful guidelines for tiered assignments (e.g., Heacox, 2001).

Table 7.1: Guidelines for Tiered Assignments

1. Select the skills that need to be taught.
2. Analyze students' readiness, learning profiles (i.e., what kind of learners they are), and interests.
3. Create an activity and place it on a continuum scale (from concrete to abstract or simple to complex) to assess its difficulty.
4. Create other activities on that scale based on the readiness of the students.
5. Match the students to the activities on this scale according to their abilities.

Ways to Organize Tiered Lessons

Tiered assignments can be organized in a variety of ways. One easy way to organize them is by using Bloom's Taxonomy (see Chapter 5). The most basic level would have activities based on knowledge and comprehension questions. Application and analysis activities would be used for the intermediate level, and the advanced level would show activities based on synthesis and evaluation. The remainder of the chapter illustrates a few of the many ways that tiered lessons can be planned and accomplished. There are various examples of how a teacher might implement tiered instruction into a classroom that includes students at various levels. You might want to read through each example and see how it could be adapted to your own classroom and content. The first example, on Harriet Tubman, utilizes Bloom's Taxonomy.

Tiered Instructional Tasks on Harriet Tubman Using Bloom's Taxonomy

Basic Level Activities:

Knowledge

How would you describe Harriet Tubman to someone meeting her for the first time in the Underground Railroad?

Comprehension

Imagine you are Harriet Tubman. Summarize your reasons for joining the Underground Railroad.

Intermediate Level Activities:

Application

Harriet Tubman used disguises to keep people from capturing her. Using props from your home, create a disguise for her to wear. Show this disguise to your classmates.

Analysis

Why do you think Harriet Tubman's husband, John, did not want her to escape slavery? List at least three possible reasons. Then, choose one reason and explain it as if you were John Tubman.

Advanced Level Activities:

Synthesis

Imagine you were Harriet Tubman's assistant conductor in the Underground Railroad. What different techniques would you use to get the runaway slaves to freedom? List at least two and then write your explanation to Harriet trying to convince her of your plan.

Evaluation

Harriet threatened the slaves that if they decided to turn back, she would shoot them. If you were Harriet, what choice would you have made to keep the slaves from turning back?

Stickers and Attributes: A Tiered Activity for Classifying Objects

Dr. Eulouise Williams, a teacher of gifted learners for more than 34 years, uses the following activity on classifying stickers as a tiered activity in her classroom. It differentiates content and process according to levels of performance and readiness. It is tiered, or parallel, because all students are working on the same skill (classifying objects), but each group is working at different levels of difficulty and complexity.

1. Select several different sets of stickers related to the same theme. Subsequent sets should have pictures with more details and complexity. For example, the teacher should include pictures with ocean themes, like seashells, sea animals, and sea plants.

2. Make a set of sticker cards by placing a different sticker on each 3x5 card. Repeat this for as many sets you need to accommodate the size of your class.

3. Divide your class into groups according to ability levels. Distribute at least one set of cards to each group. The activity will ask different groups to divide sets into two, three, or four different categories.

4. The students will examine their cards and stickers and look for details. Then they will categorize cards according to the attributes of the stickers. The above-grade level students will group stickers into four categories. The on-grade level students

will group the stickers into three categories. The below-grade level students will group the stickers into two categories.

5. Have the students complete the following tasks:

    a. Group these objects into _____ categories. (Use these headers: Name of Category and Members of Category).

    b. List as many attributes as you can which ALL of these objects possess.

    c. Of all these objects, which one is MOST DIFFERENT from the others? Why?

    d. Now, take each item and tell how it is different from all of the remaining items. Check to be sure that no other item has this identified attribute.

6. When the students have finished answering these questions, have them each find a partner and compare their work. Remind the students that sometimes others see categories that are unusual, so there might not be one right answer to the questions on their activity pages.

    (Courtesy of Dr. Eulouise Williams)

Tiered assignments can be created in centers in the classroom where students choose an activity based on what they know of their ability level. Using tiered assignments in this way encourages students to be independent. They work at their own speed and often get to choose what centers to investigate.

Projects based in centers can be ideal in a classroom with gifted students, because centers encourage them to self-initiate projects and vary the atmosphere of the typical classroom in creative ways (Smutney, 2000). Centers that offer some choice establish a learning environment that encourages gifted students to ask questions, work independently, and be creative (Berger, 1991). With the concept of centers, Tomlinson's characteristic of flexible grouping and working in many patterns within a differentiated classroom can be exemplified. Sometimes students receive whole-group instruction, sometimes the small group works together to complete a center task, and sometimes they may work independently or in pairs at their center. They are actively exploring content (Tomlinson, 1995). Each concept that a teacher introduces in centers can be broken down into three parts: basic, intermediate, and advanced. These can be labeled A for basic, B for intermediate, and C for advanced at each center.

Tiered Assignments With Math Centers

Bridget Wortman, a teacher with the North Topsail Elementary School in Hampstead, N.C., uses the following steps to tier math groups using centers in her classroom. The students rotate to various centers and find tiered levels of tasks at each center they visit.

1. Begin by assessing the class to find a basic level of understanding for every student. Use a tool that will show an understanding of curriculum areas that have been covered and are going to be covered.

2. Use the information from the assessment to place students into groups with varied levels of development so that the students can learn from one another. Be aware that the students who are low in reading may not be low in math concepts, but sometimes need help with reading directions and word problems. Keep an even number of low-, medium-, and high-level students per group as much as possible. Teach the concept to the whole class before sending students to centers to work independently.

3. When planning to teach a new concept in math, develop at least three different ways to reinforce it with center activities. Some ideas include creating

centers where students can do hands-on activities, meet one-on-one with the teacher, and transfer information to paper.

4. To create a center, break every concept down into low-, medium-, and high-level tasks. The extra work makes a huge difference when it comes to students' levels of understanding. (A helpful hint is to put the task instructions in baggies and label them easy, medium, and hard.) The students have a free choice as to which level they feel the most comfortable doing. It is important to make more activities at the various levels available than what the group may seem to need. This provides tasks for everyone if the students first pick out tasks that are too easy or too hard. They can then just choose another task at the desired level, even if everyone has already chosen task.

   a. Low—this level often has a smaller task to complete and less inquiry goes into finding the correct answer.

   b. Medium—this level has an average workload and involves some higher-level thinking skills to reach a correct answer.

   c. High—this level involves a lot of higher-level thinking skills and more math concepts that take organizational skill, and it often has a slightly larger workload than the medium group to complete.

5. Provide manipulatives for the students to use when figuring out math problems, whether they are pattern blocks for puzzles, counters for addition or subtraction, or rulers to do approximations of measurements. The students enjoy using manipulatives that link with the topic of study; for example, if the topic is the rainforest, teachers can use frogs, insects, spiders, and lizards as counters.

6. The most important center is the teacher center. At this center, the students review the concept in their groups, work with the concept, and use higher-level thinking skills to solve problems about the concept. The students answer questions, provide questions for the group, and work with a task hands-on while the teacher assesses their understanding.

(Courtesy of Bridget Wortman and North Topsail Elementary School, Hampstead, N.C.)

Figure 7.1 shows a sample weekly schedule for using math centers for tiered assignments.

Figure 7.1: Sample Weekly Schedule for Rotating Math Groups

Monday	Whole-group instruction of a new task that needs to be taught or re-taught
Tuesday, Wednesday, and Thursday	Rotating Centers a. Teacher-directed center b. Hands-on center where something is created c. Paper review center with manipulatives
Friday	Re-evaluate students—they may have a written assignment, work in math centers, or rotate around to see if they understand the concept. The teacher can plan a board game to check comprehension. There should always be another opportunity to reteach or review the information as needed.

Helpful Hints for Tiered Centers

Bridget Wortman also suggests the following tips for successful tiered centers that could be utilized for all curricular areas:

- Stick to one curriculum area on which you base all centers and differentiation, unless reviewing for a semester assessment. This keeps the focus clear and the topic the same. The students transfer the information better when they know that they are working on the same topic all week.

- Don't plan too far ahead, as you may need to reteach.

- Use resealable baggies to organize supplies for centers.

- Don't be afraid to challenge the students. They will rise to the occasion.

- Keep the groups organized. Make one child the leader of the group and make him/her responsible for the group as a whole. Not only does it provide an opportunity for students to enrich their leadership qualities, but it also provides you with a quiet, uninterrupted space of time to work in a small group. (The leader has to be the only child that is allowed to interrupt your group to ask a question.) Change the group leader once a month.

- Assessment isn't just paper and pencil. The students may be asked to create a labeled illustration or model, record information on a tape recorder, record solutions on poster paper, interview other classmates in an active participation activity with the teacher listening and monitoring, or answer oral "exit questions" before moving to the next center.

- Try to incorporate literature into your centers, if at all possible.

- Tie in a common topic that you are studying in other areas of the week. Having a thematic focus can be helpful for thinking of the tasks that the students will do.

- Always make sure that the tiered tasks are completed by the Thursday before you need them. They are often time-consuming to create, and you want to be prepared to start the centers right after you have taught the new concept.
  (Courtesy of Bridget Wortman and North Topsail Elementary School, Hampstead, N.C.)

As the chapter has explored tiered instruction and given you a few different examples from which to model your tiered lessons, the teacher of gifted students can reflect on how the differentiation process might work best in the classroom. Tiered instruction allows students at varying levels of ability to focus on the necessary concepts and skills, and yet still be challenged at the individual levels on which they are capable of working. The intent is to provide the appropriate level of instruction for the exceptional diversity of students, rather than to separate the students into leveled groups (Kingore, 2006).

Additional Resources—Tiered Lessons

Adams, C. M., & Pierce, R. L. (2006). *Differentiating instruction: A practical guide to tiered lessons in the elementary grades.* Waco, TX: Prufrock Press.

Meador, K. (2004). *Tiered activities for learning centers.* Marion, IL: Pieces of Learning.

Witherell, N. (2002). *Graphic organizers and activities for differentiated instruction in reading.* New York: Scholastic.

Chapter 7 Reflection

1. Why do you think that tiered instruction is beneficial and effective for gifted learners?

   _____

   _____

   _____

2. Explain which elements of tiered instruction you have tried in the past.

   _____

   _____

   _____

3. Describe which elements of tiered instruction you would like to put into effect in the near future.

   _____

   _____

   _____

4. Create a quick outline of a content concept that you could use for tiered instruction in your classroom. List the types of tiers you will use and the kinds of activities you will expect the students at each tier to accomplish.

   _____

   _____

   _____

   _____

Chapter Eight

Individualized Learning Contracts

Boredom due to already knowing much of the subject matter is a common problem for gifted students in the regular classroom. Teachers who are new to differentiating instruction for the gifted often find it difficult to provide everything needed for everybody. There simply are not enough hours in the day. How can teachers work with these gifted students and still provide instruction to other students in the class? This book has thus far described various strategies of differentiation in order to individualize learning for students at various ability levels. When it is necessary to provide particular learning experiences beyond the regular content for gifted students, there is a practical way that teachers can manage the separate activities chosen. Teachers can facilitate differentiation in the classroom by using individualized learning contracts (Tomlinson, 1995). Today, many colleges are utilizing independent learning contracts, but the experts also encourage them for the use of gifted students (Winebrenner & Berger, 1994). If they are organized correctly, there is every reason to believe that elementary school teachers can implement them with the gifted students in their classrooms. This chapter will discuss how learning contracts can further promote the education of gifted students.

What Are Individualized Learning Contracts?

By definition, learning contracts are *individualized*, which means they are different for each student. The term also implies that students will be *learning* something, so they will be increasing their knowledge. These learning contracts allow gifted children to broaden their learning beyond just showing mastery of the required content into actually expanding their knowledge in related areas of that same content. Finally, the word *contract* means that it is a written agreement between two people. These written agreements actively include the gifted students with the teacher in deciding and outlining what content the students will learn, what activities will be completed, in what time period, and how the learning process will be assessed (Winebrenner & Berger, 1994). Learning contracts also detail the amount of time it will take students to complete the tasks and the conditions under which they will work on their activities. Each student completes a final project to show what he/she has learned. In effect, the use of learning contracts allows gifted students to participate in designing their own learning, hopefully inspiring excitement and motivation toward their learning experiences, rather than boredom.

Why Use Individualized Learning Contracts?

Learning contracts provide structure to students while allowing them to think critically and work on complex ideas. According to an NAGC position paper, "Differentiation of Curriculum and Instruction" (1994), "appropriate educational experiences for [gifted] students are more effective when differentiated materials and activities are planned in advance and easily accessible" (para. 6). Learning contracts grant a way for the teacher to plan for their students' advanced needs in the classroom. They encourage students to develop independence and time management skills. Gifted students need to study content that is relevant to their lives, and they need activities that cause them to process meaningful ideas (Tomlinson, 1997). Options for personal interests and an element of choice are usually incorporated in the contract; students normally have the opportunity to select from a list of choices.

Learning contracts are also flexible. They can be used as enrichment options. This will help the students to delve in deeper and spend the time necessary on a topic that the class is also discussing. Contracts can also be used for acceleration if the school district is committed to continually providing the accelerated curriculum to students who need it. This all depends on the school's resources. Sometimes, gifted students need more challenges to extend past the regular content, sometimes they need to move through content more quickly, and sometimes they need more time to really delve into the full depth of a concept (Tomlinson, 1997). Learning contracts grant the teacher the structured freedom to allow that for gifted students.

How to Use Individualized Learning Contracts

Individualized learning contracts are not for everyone. The students who use these must be independent and capable of working on their own. The teachers who decide to use them should remember to customize them according to each student's needs. When used with gifted students, teachers need to consider that establishing expected outcomes for gifted students differs from establishing outcomes for the overall student population. The anticipated learning outcomes for the gifted should be consistently more demanding, broader in that they imply achieved mastery of the required content in order to undertake alternative tasks, and more focused on specific higher-level thinking activities (VanTassel-Baska, 1992).

As with curriculum compacting, the teacher can design a pretest to assess who needs an individualized learning contract. The students who score at least 80% on the pretest could be the candidates allowed to work on alternative activities under a contract. The teacher needs to create a separate contract for each participating student. The contracted students work on the alternative activities while the rest of the class is working on concepts that the contracted students have already mastered on the pretest. On each individual contract, the teachers should mark the concepts and page numbers that the students still need to master. These would be the areas in which they did not demonstrate mastery on the pretest. When the class gets to these portions of the unit, the contracted students should join the whole group for those lessons. The contracted students document their own work time. This can take the form of a log of activities that the teacher oversees and monitors. In some areas, the gifted child may not have already learned the material but still requires alternative activities in order to learn the concepts. Therefore, the child would not be able to pretest out of the overall curriculum. In these areas, the teacher would want to document on the learning contract a list of expected outcomes for the unit, the activities that the student will research independently, and an assessment of the total material to show mastery of required content (Winebrenner & Berger, 1994).

Guidelines for Setting Up a Contract

After determining who will use an individualized learning contract, the teacher needs to meet with the students to explain their contracts. Each contract must be signed by both the teacher and the student. Within the contract, there should be a set of agreed-upon rules, which represent what the teacher expects of the student as he/she works independently. The rules can include behavior issues, when and how to ask for help, attitude expectations, and where the student will be working. The teacher should also set up periodic appointments with the contracted students in order to check their progress. It is helpful if the enrichment work is self-correcting, so that the teacher won't have to spend too much time correcting papers.

Dr. Sally Reis adds that the teacher can add a process called "self-regulation," wherein the students also commit to a set of constructive behaviors that can positively affect their learning. This process is especially helpful for gifted students, who have a lack of alignment in personal potential and school performance. The students working on self-regulation add personal, behavioral, and environmental goals to their contracts. Examples of personal strategies to include would be organization of project materials and student-set goals for various components of the project. An example of a behavioral commitment includes the student deciding how to check and evaluate progress on the activity. An instance of an environmental goal is the student creating a plan for avoiding distraction while working on the contracted activities. With this addition, the students develop self-regulation of their working habits, in addition to their academic goals. They work on monitoring their performance, keeping records of their progress, and evaluating their work (Reis, 2004).

According to Susan Winebrenner and Sandra Berger, specialists in gifted education, the contract should include the concepts or outcomes that the whole class will learn (the ones that the contracted students tested out of), as well as a list of the alternative or extension activities that can be chosen by the contracted students. The teacher may decide to plan these activities alone or with the help of the students. The teacher may decide to allow the student to create the alternatives alone with teacher approval. If a contracted student does not work on his/her alternative activity or does not honor the agreed upon conditions, then he/she should be asked to rejoin the class for the rest of that unit. In these contracts, there should be some element of student choice in order to link their personal interests to the required curriculum (Winebrenner & Berger, 1994).

Because the alternative work is usually related to the unit being studied by the rest of the class, the contracted student should have the opportunity to display a product or presentation on what has been studied and learned. This will be beneficial for the entire class. Table 8.1 shows various ways for contracted students to demonstrate the end product involved in their alternative activities. For example, if a group of students were working on different extensions of one topic, they could then pull together to create a TV news broadcast where each student presents the learned concepts in a brief report. The students' final grades are a combination of activity work as well as an assessment of their mastery on the content. The students deserve high grades if the completed work represents unique and creative research, not just typical secondary sources that shows extra work at the same level as if they had been working with the whole class (Winebrenner & Berger, 1994).

Table 8.1: Final Product Ideas for Individualized Learning Contracts

video documentary	short stories/novels
radio broadcast	models
collages/posters/advertisements	puppet shows
games	essays/reports
flow charts and graphs	speeches
diaries/journals	teach a lesson
photo albums	webs/graphic organizers
interviews	illustrations/comic strips
musical jingles	newspapers
	comedy acts

Learning Contract Examples

Figures 8.1 and 8.2 show two examples of individualized learning contracts. Because contracts are individualized, the examples are different. For example, Figure 8.1 demonstrates a contract where the student is pursuing a personal interest question beyond the regular topic. The plan for the project is outlined and there are a variety of end product possibilities the student can select when completed. Figure 8.2 shows how a student is being given a choice of enrichment opportunities beyond the regular topic. The contract notes that this student is participating in alternative fraction activities in order to master the material that the rest of the class is working on with the teacher. This contract differs from the first in that it also includes behavioral goals the teacher and the student have set for the alternative activities. Following both examples is a generic blank learning contract on page 112. Teachers can study it and decide how they can adapt the ideas in this chapter to fit the needs of gifted students in their own classrooms.

Figure 8.1: Individualized Learning Contract (Sample 1)

Student's name: Bobby Williams

Topic: Civil War

Questions I have about this topic: Who are the lesser known generals of the Civil War?

Resources I can use to study this topic in more depth: History Channel videos, Internet, books from the library, and local museums

Plan for this project:

1. Begin by selecting one lesser known general from the Union and one lesser known general from the Confederacy after viewing a History Channel Civil War video
2. Use library and Internet for research
3. Prepare interview questions for historians at local university and museum
4. Pull together information in a documentary

Final project selections:

- Make a video/radio documentary
- Create a multimedia presentation
- Design mystery boxes about these two people

Project due date: February 11, 2006

Signatures:

Figure 8.2: Individualized Learning Contract (Sample 2)

Student's name: Susan Gates

Concepts still to master: multiplication of fractions, division of fractions

Chapter 6: Fractions

Page numbers: 34–36; 42–44

Enrichment choices:
- Fraction computer games dealing with multiplication and division
- Create fraction problems for a learning center
- Teach a lesson on fractions she has mastered
- Write a book about fractions

Contract rules agreed upon:
- Must wait until teacher is finished with teaching lesson before interrupting for help
- Cannot distract others in the class who are working on regular assignments
- Can search on Internet for help to problems
- Must join the class instruction for the concepts and pages written above

Signatures:

Learning contracts for alternative work "provide the basis for creating worthwhile learning experiences, for setting appropriate expectations, and for assessing the extent of learning attained" (VanTassel-Baska, 1992, p. 2). Gifted students who participate can show mastery in regular required content, and yet still extend their learning process through their interests and stretch themselves beyond their own ability levels. The teacher can now offer individualized work to highly capable students in order to challenge them, encourage their learning of new material, and relate their learning to their own interests.

Individualized Learning Contract

Name:

Topic in which I am interested:

This is what I already know about the topic:

This is what I want to learn about the topic:

Resources I can use to study this topic more in depth:

Plan for this project:
   1. Where will I find information?

   2. How will I share information?

   3. Materials I will need for my project:

Agreed upon guidelines for my independent work:

Final project selections:

Project due date:

Signatures:

Additional Resources—Individualized Learning

Greenwood, S. (2003). *On equal terms: How to make the most of learning contracts in grades 4–9.* Portsmouth, NH: Heinemann.

Martin, J. (2001). *Light bright: An activity-centered enrichment program.* Waco, TX: Prufrock Press.

Skowron, J. (2003). *Differentiated instruction: Guided and independent learning for all students.* Oak Brook, IL: Academic Services.

Williams, J. (2003). *Promoting independent learning in the primary classroom.* Philadelphia, PA: Open University Press.

Chapter 8 Reflection

1. What would you include as the necessary components of an individualized learning contract in your own classroom?

   _____

   _____

   _____

   _____

   _____

2. How can learning contracts benefit the gifted learners in your classroom?

   _____

   _____

   _____

   _____

   _____

3. Outline a contract that you might try to implement in your classroom for one of your students. Peruse the guidelines in the chapter to help you decide which components you want to include in your contract. Highlight the areas in which the student is offered the element of choice.

   _____

   _____

   _____

   _____

   _____

Creative Problem-Solving Activities

"Imagination is more than knowledge."
        –Albert Einstein

"A hunch is creativity trying to tell you something."   –Frank Capra (film director)

Many people don't see the importance of creativity. A common misconception is that a person is either creative or not creative; that is, that creativity is a natural trait that cannot be taught. Teachers often don't have the time to encourage creativity. As it is, there is very little time for core curriculum. There are a lot of misconceptions about what creativity is. Some think it only applies to those with artistic talents, which might explain why creativity is mostly ignored in schools. Is creativity really that important?

The academic experiences for children in school are based heavily on mathematical and language activities. These subjects occupy the largest time blocks of the school day and are heavily represented on state standardized tests. There is no denying that language and math are important to the learning process, but if schools only focus on these two portions of learning, they leave out a large part of the human intelligence, which includes creativity.

Many educational organizations are looking at creativity in the identification of gifted students. The Office of Gifted and Talented links typical academics with creative thinking when it describes the characteristics of creative and productive students to "include openness to experience, setting personal standards for evaluation, ability to play with ideas, willingness to take risks, preference for complexity, tolerance for ambiguity, positive self-image, and the ability to become submerged in a task" ("Giftedness and the Gifted," 1990, p. 3).

Academic abilities alone do not define the intelligence of an individual. The next chapter on Multiple Intelligences will further investigate how students have a wide array of talents and abilities. While some students might score poorly in math, they may have other strengths in areas that might go unnoticed.

This chapter will explore different models for problem solving as part of the process for developing a student's ability to think creatively. First, you will have a chance to examine various definitions of the term *creativity*. As the chapter connects creativity to problem solving, you will be introduced to various models for posing problem solving to gifted students. You will be introduced to Wallas' Method of creative thinking (Wallas, 1926), which highlights four steps that people go through in solving problems. The chapter will also introduce the Two-Step Method (Davis, 1998) of forming big ideas and elaborating on them. Finally, it will examine the Creative Problem-Solving Model (Osborn, 1963) and how it helps students brainstorm many ideas and choose the best ones.

Connecting Creativity and Problem Solving

First, let's try to define creativity. Most people say that creativity is the ability to produce something original. Educator Paul Torrance (1986) defines creativity as fluency, flexibility, originality, and sometimes elaboration. In May of 1999, the National Advisory Committee on Creative and Cultural Education issued a report titled, *All Our Futures: Creativity, Culture, and Education* (1999). In this report, creativity is defined as the "imaginative activity fashioned so as to produce outcomes that are both original and of value" (Section 28). According to Gary Davis, a specialist in the field of gifted education, creativity extends past the idea of just thinking of a lot of ideas. He believes that creative thinking is a way of life and a characteristic of one's personality. Creativity can be in one's world perspective or in the way someone interacts with others. Davis continues to articulate that people who live creatively need to develop their talents and potential. He urges people to become who they are capable of becoming and to explore new places and new ideas. Davis reminds his readers that creative people should be sensitive to the problems of others (Davis, 1998). Under these definitions, everyone has the ability to be creative. The more students are given the chance to develop their creativity, the more creative they will become. In the realm of creativity, practice makes perfect.

One way to develop students' creativity is to give them problems to solve. Think about the last problem you encountered. Did you find the best solution? Were you motivated to try different solutions? What if you would have done something differently? Creativity is essential for human survival. Daily life is a major arena for authentic creative problem solving. Problems abound everywhere we look. They are in the workplace and at home. Problems arise as children play at recess or try to work together on a classroom project. There are problems in families and within friendships. Teachers need to coach their students in how to effectively approach many of these problems. Teachers can accomplish these goals through teaching various problem-solving strategies.

Why Use Creative Problem Solving With Gifted Students?

There is an automatic connection between problem solving and gifted students. Research shows that gifted children are better at problem solving than average students (Runco, 1986). In fact, it was found that gifted students mimic the behaviors of experts while problem solving; this includes the strategies they used to solve problems (Rogers, 1986). Many gifted children also possess certain identified creative talents. These particulars create a natural motivation to further cultivate creative problem solving with gifted children. All students can benefit from opportunities to problem solve, but gifted students, in particular, benefit. While problem solving, gifted students learn thinking skills more quickly and apply them to new situations more often than average students (Carr & Borkowski, 1987). This research suggests that gifted children have an advantage (in comparison with their peers) in developing problem-solving strategies.

Gifted students need opportunities to develop their personal creative-thinking techniques so that they can effectively solve problems. Some basic tips include: asking your students to keep an idea-and-solution journal to record their ideas and solutions; encouraging them to take walks outside and to observe what they see; facilitating their interaction with others who are creative; and assigning reading texts about creative individuals such as inventors from the past. Beyond these guidelines, a teacher of gifted children must also show them different ways to solve problems. The remainder of the chapter will explore various methods utilized for creatively solving problems.

The Wallas Method

Often, solving problems can involve deliberate steps. This is shown in various creative problem-solving methods. One method was created by Graham Wallas (1926) and is called the Wallas Model for the Process of Creativity. Using Wallas' Model, the problem solver does not have to use every step listed, nor does he/she have to always go in a particular order. Listed below are Wallas' steps for problem solving.

1. **Preparation:** In this step, the problem finders look for all the information they can find. They gather data, look at available materials, and review research.

2. **Incubation:** Problem finders allow their unconscious minds to work. This step is mysterious, but Wallas said that it occurred when the problem finder interacted away from the problem topic (like jogging, playing sports, watching TV, eating tacos, taking a shower, etc.). During this stage, the focus is taken away from mentally working on the problem.

3. **Illumination:** This is the "Aha!" moment. There is a sudden light that goes on in one's head where a solution appears. It usually appears after some time is spent away from the problem. The unconscious mind is working on the problem and the answer can come while jogging, sleeping, showering, etc.

4. **Verification:** This step involves the problem finder checking to make sure their solution really works. If not, the steps can be repeated over again.

Table 9.1 shows the potential progress involved in following the steps of the Wallas Method while working on solving a problem. For each step, possible problem-solving activities are revealed.

Table 9.1: Sample Problem Solving Using the Wallas Method

Step	Description of Problem-Solving Process
Preparation	• Immerse yourself in the problem • Brainstorm ideas • Feel a bit of frustration • Think hard
Incubation	• Let the problem simmer • Allow the unconscious mind to be the storehouse for everything you know
Illumination	• "Aha!" moment arrives • The solution comes to you
Verification	• Put it to use to see if it works • If not, go back to step 1

The Two-Stage Model

One model of problem solving involves just two steps. It is called the Two-Stage Model (Davis, 1998). The first step is the **big idea** stage and involves a person actively looking for a new idea. This idea is usually found by using creative thinking like brainstorming or analogies. The second stage is the **elaboration** stage. This stage is when a person develops the idea, elaborates on the idea, and finally implements the idea. The materials are pulled together, sketches are created, and the final work is completed. For example, a student writer will create the plot and characters and then write his novel. Creativity is not only needed to get the big idea, but it is needed to carry out the plans to make the big idea work. While this may seem like a relatively simple plan for problem solving, teachers must keep in mind that even gifted students need modeling of strategies, explicit instruction in how to use them in learning, and plenty of opportunities to practice using them before the students can use them independently and appropriately in learning situations.

Creative Problem Solving

Another method, called the Creative Problem-Solving Model (CPS), was developed by Alex Osborn and Sidney Parnes in the 1960s. Since then, the model has been refined. Within each step, the problem solver engages in divergent thinking as he/she generates many ideas. Then, the problem solver engages in convergent thinking as he/she selects the best ideas. While the Wallas Method involves finding solutions to problems that arise in everyday life, the CPS Model provides an effective way for teachers to choose hypothetical problems and then guide their students through creative ways of solving those problems. Therefore, this becomes a useful technique for developing the skills of creative problem solving in students (Osborn, 1963).

Table 9.2 shows the steps for the CPS model.

Table 9.2: Steps for the CPS Model

1. **Objective (Mess) Finding:** Select a problem.
2. **Fact Finding:** List what you know about the problem.
3. **Problem Finding:** Ask, "In what ways might we. . ." questions. What is the real problem? Find out the real objective.
4. **Idea Finding:** Brainstorm ideas about step 2.
5. **Solution Finding:** List criteria to evaluate your ideas and select your best idea.
6. **Acceptance Finding**: Find ways of putting the best ideas into action.

Students can use the CPS model to help them solve authentic problems in their schools, like keeping the hallways free of trash or funding a healthier lunch menu.

The chart on page 124 provides a blank format for a student to use in order to organize the creative process involved in identifying the best ideas for a problem. Teachers can guide the students through the CPS process, coaching them through each step.

Real everyday problems arise without having to go search for them. Teachers can effectively prepare students to address those problems by giving them practice with theoretical problems that imitate real situations. Additionally, practice with imaginary problems (like the alien example below) could help students think more creatively in solving those problems as they offer inspiration and inventiveness. Ideas for creative problem solving can come from television, newspaper articles, or literature, just to name a few. Because students bring their own prior knowledge to develop ideas and then formulate those ideas into hypotheses, these scenarios can be used with most any age group. The students at the high school level will invariably produce a deeper investigation with more complex results than will the students in an elementary classroom.

Possible problems to solve creatively:

1. An alien wants to take over your mind.

2. You have just found a wallet with $100,000 in it.

3. You have to babysit the worst children in the neighborhood for five hours.

4. You are in charge of choosing a book that everyone will like for your new book club.

5. The water in your town is not fit to drink.

6. You are chosen to set up a fire prevention plan for your neighborhood.

7. Gangs are destroying your home's fence with graffiti.

8. You have too much homework.

9. A student in your class is disrespectful to others.

10. You have been chosen to run for student council president.

Additional Resources—Creative Problem Solving

Draze, D. (2005). *Creative problem solving for kids.* Waco, TX: Prufrock Press.

Treffinger, D. (1980). *Encouraging creative learning for the gifted and talented.* Ventura, CA: National State Leadership Training.

Treffinger, D. (2000). *Practice problems for creative problem solving.* Waco, TX: Prufrock Press.

Creative Problem Solving Organizer

Directions: Use the chart to help organize your problem solving.

Objective (Mess) Finding	Fact Finding	Problem Finding	Idea Finding	Solution Finding	Acceptance Finding	Examples to Use for Creative Problem Solving

Chapter 9 Reflection

1. How do you perceive creativity as linked with the problem-solving process?

   _____

   _____

   _____

   _____

   _____

2. What is a teacher's role in helping students further develop creative problem solving?

   _____

   _____

   _____

   _____

   _____

3. Of the methods introduced in Chapter 9, which one could you use in your classroom and how would you present it?

   _____

   _____

   _____

   _____

   _____

Multiple Intelligences

> We are not all the same; we do not all have the
> same kinds of minds; education works most
> effectively for most individuals if these differ-
> ences . . . are taken into account rather than
> denied or ignored. (Gardner, 1995, p. 208)

This statement by Howard Gardner is especially true
within the gifted population. Gifted students have an
assortment of ways in which they can best demonstrate
their intelligence. Contrary to popular belief, not all
gifted students enjoy writing stories, for example. Some
prefer to express themselves through art. Others desire
to use their hands to design spatial objects, like maps
and diagrams. There are a few who enjoy doing things
musically or kinesthetically with their bodies. As this
chapter will discuss, teachers of gifted students should

give an interest inventory to find out the natural talents and gifts of the gifted students in their classrooms. Once teachers discover where their students' strengths and weaknesses are found, they can be inspired to offer gifted students activities that engage and celebrate their natural talents and gifts.

Using the Multiple Intelligences Model is an effective way to accommodate gifted students' learning styles and preferences. As students possess different abilities and talents in varying degrees (multiple intelligences), there are also different ways in which they most straightforwardly learn (commonly referred to as learning styles). Some compare the modern-day education system to an industrial plant where everyone is doing the same thing at the same time. When the end of the day comes, it is expected that all the products should be the same. However, research shows that students have different preferences and interests that are influenced by their distinct talents and abilities. The Multiple Intelligences Model provides an avenue for gifted students (and all students, for that matter) to express their creativity through the products they produce. Teachers can encourage students to utilize their more developed intelligences to help them understand a subject that might generally make use of their weaker intelligences (Brualdi, 1996). Students then have the chance to choose activities based on their own interests, strengths, and unique capabilities.

What Are Multiple Intelligences?

The Multiple Intelligences Model is based on the renowned 1983 book *Frames of Mind: The Theory of Multiple Intelligences* by one primary researcher named Howard Gardner. His research, which argues that there are differences between reason, intelligence, logic, and knowledge, expanded the concept of intelligence to include other areas such as music, spatial relations, and the understanding of feelings and intentions (Brualdi, 1996). Gardner originally identified seven intelligences, which include: verbal/linguistic; logical/mathematical; bodily/kinesthetic; intrapersonal; interpersonal; musical/rhythmic; and visual/spatial. He later added the eighth intelligence, the naturalist intelligence, and often considers adding an existential intelligence, which he describes as the "intelligence of big questions," as well as others in the future (Gardner, 2003). He says that everyone possesses each of these intelligences, but some intelligences are more developed than others. Each person has an individual profile which is made up of strengths and weaknesses in the various areas of intelligence (Gardner, 2003). Twenty years after his original work in multiple intelligences, Gardner states: "I decided to call these faculties 'multiple intelligences' rather than abilities or gifts. This seemingly minor lexical substitution proved very important; I am quite confident that if I had written a book called 'Seven Talents' it would not have received the attention that *Frames of Mind* received" (Gardner, 2003, p. 3).

Teaching the curriculum with multiple intelligences in mind allows for the development of multiple paths of instruction and multiple student products that encourage students' strengths and also build up their weaknesses. Many educators have come to think of multiple intelligences as a way to encourage the learning process as children learn; it provides avenues by which all students can achieve success. A major implication is that teachers should organize their instruction to identify and teach toward a broad spectrum of types of intelligences. This then triggers the wide variety of intelligences in a classroom and facilitates deeper understanding of content for more students (Brualdi, 1996). For the teachers of gifted students, the use of multiple intelligences can help bring out their students' advanced natural talents as they learn the required content in challenging and engaging ways appropriate for gifted learners.

The Eight Intelligences

As you read through the following descriptions, please remember that Gardner's theory says that everyone has a combination of all of the intelligences. "Nevertheless, all students will come into the classroom with different sets of developed intelligences. This means that each child will have his own unique set of intellectual strengths and weaknesses" (Brualdi, 1996, p. 4). The theory of multiple intelligences applies to all children, although gifted students may exhibit extraordinary strengths in some of these areas. Therefore, a teacher should help gifted students understand in which areas they are strongest and then allow them to use these strengths while they address all their learning, whether it is through enrichment activities, acceleration activities, or other projects listed on individualized learning contracts. While each intelligence clearly has advantages for students in the subject area closest to that intelligence (for example, the logical/mathematical intelligence and any math subject), each of the following descriptions will highlight how strength in that area can aid a gifted student across all curricular areas through their specialized content and alternative learning activities.

Verbal/Linguistic Intelligence

Students with a strong verbal/linguistic intelligence are usually described as bookworms. They enjoy good stories and spend lots of time with their noses in a book. They have good memories, too. They often like to rewrite the ends of stories, compose poetry, and create riddles or jokes. They like to decode words and look for hidden meanings. They are good speakers and get a kick out of debating a topic with others. If they get the chance, they would probably make great storytellers. A famous person with the verbal/linguistic intelligence was Theodor Seuss Geisel, otherwise known as Dr. Seuss. He flooded children's libraries with his creative style of rhyming words with humor. Gifted students with this intelligence can use their strength in words to write detailed reports or give presentations to summarize their alternative assignments across all subject areas. These students should be given real-life issues to research, form opinions of topics, and debate issues with others.

Logical/Mathematical Intelligence

Students with a strong logical/mathematical intelligence are math people. They like to ask questions about how things work. Sometimes they even take things apart to see how they were put together. They can do most math problems quickly in their heads and enjoy math games that have to do with counting. They also like to create their own strategies for solving problems or playing games. Logic puzzles and brainteasers are fun for them, and they enjoy challenging their brains. A famous person with the logical/mathematical intelligence was Albert Einstein. He contributed to the study of physics and mathematics. Logically- and mathematically-excelling gifted students might be motivated by creating charts in order to schedule assignment pacing and progress. Authentic problem solving will be necessary in any research project these gifted students are given. In some curricular areas, they might be challenged to create games and puzzles that help other students learn the content.

Bodily/Kinesthetic Intelligence

Students with a strong bodily/kinesthetic intelligence are athletic and excel easily in at least one sport. They move constantly and twitch, tap, and fidget if they have to sit still for very long. They like taking things apart and putting them back together. They also like to touch everything they see. They like to play with clay and enjoy simple things like finger painting. If they watch videotapes of themselves, they might find that they are always jumping or running around. A famous person with the bodily/kinesthetic intelligence is Michael Jordan. He was voted the #1 athlete of the twentieth century. He is by far the greatest basketball player of all time and led his team, the Chicago Bulls, to victory even though he was sick with the flu.

Obviously, gifted students with great strength in this area will need to be actively constructing in their alternative learning projects through all the curricular areas. For example, while researching an ancient society, they might make a model of a typical city in that society. These students might need some literal walking time as they work on the solutions to problems that they are trying to decipher. Bodily movement will often be a necessity for mental processing.

Intrapersonal Intelligence

Students with a strong intrapersonal intelligence know themselves very well—they know their strengths and weaknesses. Each day they like to spend time alone thinking and often like to write their thoughts in journals and diaries. They would rather work alone than with a group of students. They are independent and feel good about themselves. They also know how to learn from their own failures and successes. A famous person with the intrapersonal intelligence was Charles Schultz, who created the Peanuts cartoons. He was always thinking, living, and breathing the life of his cartoons. He identified with all of his Peanuts characters and drew cartoons that dealt with his own fears, insecurities, dreams, and experiences.

Gifted students who demonstrate a high skill in this intelligence area will obviously enjoy working on their enrichment or acceleration activities on their own. They will need to keep careful logs to analyze how their time is spent. Teachers will need to be sensitive to the fact that these students will need some support in activities where they are required to work with others, whether it is with other gifted students or not. They might need an out-of-the-ordinary task within the group project; this might help them maintain some of their autonomy while they learn to work cooperatively.

Interpersonal Intelligence

Students with a strong interpersonal intelligence like to socialize, and they normally have many friends and enjoy being around others. They are also natural leaders. People look to them for decisions and leadership. They are good with helping friends solve problems. They are especially good at showing concern for other people. Playing games with friends is one of their favorite things to do, and they like to belong to clubs or groups. A famous person with the interpersonal intelligence was Princess Diana of Wales. She spoke up for others in need; whether it was someone dying of AIDS or a child in the hospital, she expressed compassion and volunteered her time to raise awareness and money.

Interpersonal gifted students might have a hard time working on the alternative curriculum requiring independence. The teacher can make use of this particular strength by allowing them to be part of the leadership process of delegating tasks for all of the students working on learning contracts. It is important to note that students with interpersonal or intrapersonal strengths cannot always have "their way" in a classroom. They need to learn to work in both types of situations. Therefore, interpersonal students will need more teacher support in the activities they have to complete alone. Perhaps the teacher can allow a sharing time for these students, rather than an independent log, where they can communicate with others about how they spent their independent learning time.

Musical/Rhythmic Intelligence

Students with a strong musical/rhythmic intelligence are music people. They are often very sensitive to noise.

As a result, they know when music is off-key. They are good at remembering melodies and rhythms. They might even play an instrument or sing in a choir. When they work, they tap their feet or pencils to rhythms in their heads. If they ever get the chance, they like going to concerts. Someday, they might even want to write their own songs or melodies. A famous person with the musical intelligence was Elvis Presley. He changed history with his controversial rock-and-roll style of music during the 1950s.

Gifted students who excel in this area hopefully are getting the chance to nurture it outside of school. However, the teacher can still encourage them to use their musical and rhythmic skills in their final learning products that they present to the class. By having the opportunity to rework concepts into songs, poetry, raps, and musical collections, they can employ their talent and reinforce content concepts.

Visual/Spatial Intelligence

Students with a strong visual/spatial intelligence think in pictures. They are especially good at reading maps, charts, and diagrams, and they may spend lots of time daydreaming, too. They like putting together puzzles and solving mazes. Art activities are among their favorite in school. They often doodle pictures in class. They understand more when there are pictures to go along with a presentation or reading sample. A famous person with a strong spatial intelligence is Ralph Lauren. He is a famous designer whose trademark is famous around the world. His designer fabrics reach beyond all age barriers and have a casual "American" appeal.

Gifted students with exceptional propensity toward this area should have the chance to use visuals in their research and make them in their presentations of learning across all curricular areas. They should explore primary sources of visual information and find ways to present information visually in the classroom. In group activities, they can help illustrate ideas. In technology-based projects, they can use desktop publishing software.

Naturalist Intelligence

Students with a strong naturalist intelligence like the outdoors. They love spending time in nature and often like to camp. They are good with animals and might even have several pets at home. When walking outside, they know which direction is North, South, and so on. Weather interests them, and if they have the chance, they spend it watching The Weather Channel on television. They like looking at nature magazines and reading books about animals. They might even have a great fossil collection. A famous person with the naturalist intelligence was Steve Irwin, best known as the "crocodile hunter." Steve spent his entire life studying, living, and working with animals. Steve and his wife Terri traveled around the world helping to educate the public about the care and responsibility we all have to the natural world.

Teachers should encourage gifted students who have a strong inclination toward nature to bring naturalist issues, such as conservation, animal care and rights, and weather issues, into their studies across mathematical, historical, and scientific themes. They might also guide class projects that can be explored around the school or take leadership roles on field trips.

How to Use Multiple Intelligences for Gifted Learners

Finding out the intelligence profile for each of your gifted students is just the first step. Teachers should teach their students and their parents about these intelligences as well. This can be done in a variety of ways.

After having students take a multiple intelligences inventory test (see page 139), some teachers distribute descriptions of the intelligences and have their students learn more about their strengths in the various areas. The teacher can then help them choose the area or areas where they think they are strongest in order to then form groups according to one of their strengths. Each group creates a poster for one of their top intelligences and then presents it to the class as a mini lesson about that intelligence. These posters serve as reminders of the different intelligences and can also be used as markers for centers and stations within classrooms. The gifted students with these strengths should be encouraged to add tips for the other students about how they can strengthen their profile in that realm of intelligence. These tips can be followed if a student wants to widen his/her intelligence range across the various areas.

On the posters, the gifted students should also brainstorm and record ways that the teacher can recognize their intelligences across the various curricular areas. For example, a verbal/linguistic student might record that he/she wants to give an oral presentation instead of taking a multiple-choice test. A kinesthetic learner in a math class might ask to use manipulatives in order to solve problems. This will give students the sense that the teacher is interested in allowing them to express their intelligences sincerely. These activities not only help students respect the diversity in the classroom, they also help the students to understand one another, as well as themselves, better. As projects arise, the students will know who to go to for help, in addition to how to help someone who is struggling.

Next, classroom curriculum can be changed to fit the students' needs. Many teachers offer activities in various lessons as choices, centers/stations, or for independent study. It is important to remember that not all intelligences can be in every lesson every day. Realistically, a lesson can contain opportunities for students to display their intelligence across two or three different multiple intelligence activities, while a day or week of stations and centers can offer activities based on all the intelligences. In a classroom with gifted learners, the theory of multiple intelligences offers a lot of exciting possibilities because so many gifted learners are working on extensions of content, faster pacing of the material, and individualized learning contracts. These extensions provide many opportunities to be active explorers of materials with the strengths that each of the gifted students bring to their projects. Furthermore, a teacher should assess his/her own assessment procedures. Teachers tend to give assessments according to the way that they themselves like to be assessed. For example, verbal/linguistic teachers tend to love to give essay assessments. If the teacher is always asking the gifted students to write a report after a contracted project, and one student is stronger in the musical/rhythmic area, then this student is not being given the opportunity to demonstrate mastery of concepts in his/her most intelligent way.

Page 139 contains a sample student Multiple Intelligences Inventory Test. Many teachers have their students answer questions on inventory tests similar to this one. Section 1 describes the verbal/linguistic student; section 2 describes the logical/mathematical student; section 3 describes the bodily/kinesthetic student; section 4 describes the intrapersonal student; section 5 describes the interpersonal student; section 6 describes the musical/rhythmic student; section 7 describes the visual/spatial student; and section 8 describes the naturalistic student.

The students should take the test independently, marking each question with a yes or no answer. For each section, they need to total their yes answers. The teacher should then provide a general description of each area and give them the opportunity to look at their top three sections and evaluate which they think is their strongest area. As all teachers know, no single measure is completely accurate, so a student may decide that his/her second highest score is really the area where they feel they demonstrate the most strength. Gifted students could be charged with the assignment of giving themselves a percentage score for each of the eight intelligences (for example, 30% logical/mathematical, 15% naturalist, etc.), so that the final score equals "100% intelligent." As Gardner himself poses the possibilities of further intelligences, gifted students should have the opportunity to articulate further areas in which they feel that they are gifted. Perhaps they could be given the assignment of writing a persuasive letter to Gardner to include that new intelligence area. Gardner notes that he is actually quite surprised at how much attention his theory has had in the educational field (Gardner, 2003). Here are some sample questions the teacher could pose in order to have students identify their greatest strengths. The teacher needs to emphasize that the students have varying abilities in many of the areas, and that the students can strive to strengthen their scores and abilities in any of the areas.

- If you had two hours after school to do anything (and your television isn't working!), what would you choose to do?
- If you could teach your best friend how to do something, what would it be?
- If I were going to have you research _____, how would you want to present to the class what you learned?

Sample Multiple Intelligences Inventory Test

	Questions	Yes	No
Section 1	Do you like to write poetry or stories?		
	Do you have a journal or a diary in which you write?		
	Do you like solving crossword puzzles or creating tongue twisters?		
	Do you enjoy debating?		
	Would you like to write a script for a TV show?		
	Would you enjoy telling stories to a younger class?		
	Section 1 TOTAL:		
Section 2	Do you enjoy solving math problems and/or analogies?		
	Do you like to play counting games?		
	Do you enjoy writing math story problems?		
	Do you like to play checkers or chess?		
	Do you like finding measurements for things?		
	Do you enjoy making graphs to show information?		
	Section 2 TOTAL:		
Section 3	Do you enjoy playing sports?		
	Would you ever want to learn sign language?		
	Do you like exercising or hiking?		
	Do you enjoy acting out plays?		
	Do you feel like you need to move your body all the time?		
	Do you enjoy dancing?		
	Section 3 TOTAL:		
Section 4	Do you keep a diary or a journal?		
	Do you like setting goals for yourself?		
	Do you spend time thinking about your work?		
	Would you ever like to write an autobiography?		
	Do you spend lots of time thinking quietly?		
	Do you need to spend time alone everyday?		
	Section 4 TOTAL:		
Section 5	Do you like playing games with friends?		
	Do you enjoy doing class work with a group of people?		
	Would you want to interview someone important?		
	Do you like conducting surveys?		
	Are you good at solving problems between people?		
	Do you like being around lots of people?		
	Section 5 TOTAL:		
Section 6	Would you enjoy writing an advertising jingle for a product?		
	Do you play an instrument?		
	Is it easy for you to think of sound effects to add to a story to make it more interesting?		
	Do you pick up tunes and rhythms easily?		
	Would you ever like to write your own song?		
	Do you enjoy going to concerts?		
	Section 6 TOTAL:		
Section 7	Do you like putting together puzzles?		
	Do you enjoy drawing or painting?		
	Would you enjoy creating or reading a map of your neighborhood?		
	Do you like playing board games?		
	Would you like to create a video of an important event?		
	Would you ever want to design a sculpture?		
	Section 7 TOTAL:		
Section 8	Do you like to watch The Weather Channel or study the forecast in the paper?		
	Do you enjoy spending time outdoors?		
	Do you read books or magazines about nature?		
	Would you ever want to be a veterinarian?		
	Are you good at telling directions?		
	Do you like animals and wish you had many pets?		
	Section 8 TOTAL:		

Parent Introduction to Multiple Intelligences

When teachers are discussing multiple intelligences in the classroom or forming alternative project-based activities for gifted students based on their strengths, it would be wise to inform the parents about the process. Page 141 contains a sample letter that describes Gardner's theory, why it is being applied to a particular classroom and students, and how parents can encourage the strengths their children possess. It also notes that parents can foster activities in some of the areas that their children might not be as strong.

Dear Parents,

It is important that all students are learning in our classroom. In 1983, an educational psychologist named Howard Gardner identified what he termed "Multiple Intelligences" in his book *Frames of Mind: The Theory of Multiple Intelligences*. Educators today use multiple intelligences to help them understand their students and plan lessons accordingly. We are on a quest to make sure everyone in our classroom is learning at full capacity. Not everyone comes with the same strengths and weaknesses when they learn. Students in our classroom show a variety of talents. They might be good at reading and writing, talented with numbers and logic, natural-born leaders, and budding artists. Others need to move around, some are musical, and a few have a connection with nature. All students show a different combination of all of these descriptions.

Once each student knows where his/her strengths are found, he/she can use that information to learn more efficiently in all areas. The students have taken an inventory test to identify their strengths and weaknesses in these various areas. Then they read material that helped them to understand how they can apply them to their learning preferences. Talk with your child about where he/she feels strongest. Discuss in which areas your child would like to expand and help your child develop a plan to work on the weaker areas.

Below you will find a summary of the eight different multiple intelligences.

The Verbal/Linguistic child thinks in words. He/she likes to write, read, play word games, and tell interesting stories. He/she enjoys diaries, books, and writing materials.

The Logical/Mathematical child thinks by reasoning. He/she likes figuring out problems, puzzles, experimenting, and calculating. He/she enjoys trips to museums and using science supplies and math manipulatives.

The Bodily/Kinesthetic child thinks by using his/her body. He/she likes dancing, moving, jumping, running, and touching. He/she enjoys movement, sports, theater, physical games, and hands-on activities.

The Intrapersonal child keeps his/her thoughts to him/herself. He/she likes to set goals, daydream, and to be in quiet places. He/she enjoys having time alone and working on individualized projects.

The Interpersonal child thinks by talking about his/her ideas with others. He/she likes organizing events, being the leader, socializing, and mediating between friends. He/she enjoys time with friends, group projects, and social events.

The Musical/Rhythmic child thinks in melodies and rhythms. He/she likes listening to music, making his/her own music, tapping to the rhythm, and singing. He/she may enjoy playing a musical instrument, going to concerts, or singing along with a karaoke machine.

The Visual/Spatial child thinks in pictures. He/she likes to draw, design, and doodle. He/she enjoys art supplies, building materials, video equipment, and puzzles.

The Naturalistic child thinks by classifying. He/she likes studying anything in nature, including rocks, animals, plants, and the weather. He/she enjoys time outside, nature hikes, telescopes, binoculars, and writing in notebooks for classification.

Thank you,

_____

Your child's teacher

Multiple Intelligences Newspaper Activities

This section demonstrates how one activity with newspapers can be expanded to meet the various intelligences identified for gifted students. If students come with various strengths, then activities such as these will help them highlight and further reinforce their favorite ways of demonstrating their intelligence. These newspaper activities can be applied to any grade-level appropriate newspapers. They could be applied to a whole-class reading of the newspaper with various activities for assessment of understanding, or they could be applied to centers activities with newspapers.

Verbal/Linguistic

Look at a picture from the newspaper, but don't look at the caption. What questions do you have about this photo? Brainstorm a list of at least five questions. Then read the caption. Does it answer any of your questions? Write a story about this photo based on the information you now know.

Logical/Mathematical

Imagine the newspaper asked you to write a brainteaser for tomorrow's edition. What would you create? Write this teaser and don't forget to include the answer on the backside for easy checking.

Bodily/Kinesthetic

Create a game that uses the newspaper and a spinner. Make a list of rules and then demonstrate it for your class.

Intrapersonal

Find a comic strip character that has a problem. Then create a step-by-step plan for that person to work through his/her problem.

Interpersonal

Work with another person to create a live broadcast of a story from the newspaper. You can both share in reporting the story, or one of you can be the anchorman and the other the reporter on the scene.

Musical/Rhythmic

Select five stories from the newspaper. Then find a theme song to go along with each story with an explanation of why it is a good song for the story.

Visual/Spatial

Read a story from the newspaper. Then draw a picture to go along with that story for the newspaper.

Naturalist

Look at the newspaper weather predictions for one week. Are the predictions for the daily highs and lows correct? Make a graph that shows the predictions with what actually happens.

Multiple Intelligences State History Activities

State history is often studied in elementary schools. Here you will see various activities across the different intelligence areas where students could demonstrate their own strongest intelligences as they learn the content.

Verbal/Linguistic

Study the life of a person who made a big contribution within the history of your state. Write an acrostic poem about this person describing what he/she did for your state.

Logical/Mathematical

Make a timeline that shows the events surrounding this person's life. Be sure to include the important things this person did for your state on this timeline.

Bodily/Kinesthetic

Create a charades game about this person for your class. Include at least five charades cards for your game. Introduce this game and play it with your class.

Intrapersonal

Imagine you knew this person who did so much for your state. Write about an important event in which this person was involved as if you were there.

Interpersonal

Work with other people to create an interview for a television show with this person and others who knew him/her. Conduct this interview in front of your class.

Musical/Rhythmic

Write a song that would sum up the things this person did for your state. Sing this song for your teacher.

Visual/Spatial

Create a multimedia presentation about this famous person. Be sure to include the important things this person did for your state.

Naturalist

Build a miniature model of a monument to honor this person's work for your state. Decide on an outdoor location to place this monument. Be sure to write a plaque to explain the monument's meaning.

Additional Resources—Multiple Intelligences

Fasko, D. (2001, April). An analysis of multiple intelligences theory and its use with the gifted and talented. *Roeper Review 23(3)*, 126–130.

Willard-Holt, C. (1998). *Applying multiple intelligences to gifted education: I'm not just an IQ score!* Manassas, VA: Gifted Education Press.

Chapter 10 Reflection

1. What are some ways that you allow your gifted students to demonstrate their intelligence in different ways?

_____

_____

_____

_____

2. How can you vary assessment practices in the classroom in order to give different gifted students the opportunities to succeed according to their intelligences?

_____

_____

_____

_____

3. What is a unit of study your students will participate in this year? What are various activities you can plan across the multiple intelligences that can allow each of your students to practice their various levels of intelligence?

_____

_____

_____

_____

Glossary

acceleration—when gifted students are provided with the opportunity to advance through the curriculum at a fast pace

analysis—when students break information into parts by identifying causes and motives

application—when students apply the facts, knowledge, and techniques they have learned to new situations

Bloom's Taxonomy of Cognitive Thought—a list developed by Benjamin Bloom that categorizes learning skills into the following six categories: knowledge, comprehension, application, analysis, synthesis, and evaluation

bodily/kinesthetic intelligence—the ability to use movement for learning

complexity—coined by Sandra Kaplan; stresses the relationship between disciplines and how these relationships have changed over time, and it uses a variety of perspectives when looking at issues; in content or subject matter, it exists in three main elements: over time, multiple perspectives, and interdisciplinary relationships

comprehension—when students show their understanding of facts and ideas by translating, comparing, organizing, and stating the main ideas

content—the processes and knowledge that students learn in school

creative problem solving—the set of six stages used to solve problems and find new ideas

curriculum compacting—a method of summarizing and condensing curriculum that students have already mastered

depth—coined by Sandra Kaplan; when students explore a topic from concrete to abstract ideas, from the familiar to unfamiliar concepts, and from known to unknown facts, and they elaborate on content and engage in the investigation of new ideas and concepts

differentiate—a process by which curriculum is modified to meet the needs of all learners in a classroom

enrichment—when gifted students are provided with activities that provide a greater depth and breadth to the topic they are studying. These activities are typically more complex than the regular activities planned for standards based content.

evaluation—when students make and defend their opinions about information, ideas, and quality based on criteria

gifted and talented—terms usually attributed to intellectually talented people who excel in defined areas and are identified to receive special program services in the school; each state has its own definition for identification purposes

giftedness—a trait usually attributed to intelligence found in people from all cultural and ethnic backgrounds who exhibit a high level of talent

individualized learning contracts—exclusive written agreements between the teacher and student by which the student independently studies a topic and produces a project based on what he/she has learned from his/her research

interpersonal intelligence—the ability to understand the feelings and intentions of others

intrapersonal intelligence—the ability to understand one's own feelings and motivations

knowledge—the lowest level of Bloom's Taxonomy that involves the basic facts, terms, concepts, and answers

logical/mathematical intelligence—the ability to reason deductively and think logically

Multiple Intelligences Model—a theory that states all people possess at least eight different kinds of intelligences: verbal/linguistic, logical/mathematical, visual/spatial, bodily/kinesthetic, musical/rhythmic, interpersonal, intrapersonal, and naturalist

musical/rhythmic intelligence—the ability to recognize and compose musical tones, rhythms, and pitches

naturalist intelligence—the ability to classify natural phenomena and have an ongoing curiosity and knowledge of the natural world

problem solving—the conscious steps a person takes to solve a problem

process—the procedure or course of action taken to learn about a topic

product—the tangible result produced by a student that shows what he/she has learned about a topic

scaffolding—same as tiered assignments, wherein a lesson is differentiated to at least three different levels to meet the needs of all students

synthesis—when students compile information in various ways and present a new solution or pattern

tiered assignments—when a lesson is differentiated to at least three different levels to meet the needs of all students

verbal/linguistic intelligence—involves the love of books and writing

visual/spatial intelligence—the ability to create mental images and pictures in order to solve problems

References

Berger, S. (1991). *Differentiating curriculum for gifted students*. Reston, VA: ERIC Clearinghouse on Handicapped and Gifted Children. (ERIC Document Reproduction Service No. ED342175)

Bloom, B. S., Englehart, M. D., Furst, E. J., Hill, W. H., & Krathwohl, D. R. (1956). *Taxonomy of educational objectives: The classification of educational goals*. New York: Longmans, Green.

Brualdi, A. C. (1996). *Multiple intelligences: Gardner's theory*. Washington, DC: ERIC Clearinghouse on Assessment and Evaluation. (ERIC Document Reproduction Service No. ED410226)

Brualdi, A. C. (2001). *Classroom questions*. Washington, DC: ERIC Clearinghouse on Assessment and Evaluation. (ERIC Document Reproduction Service No. ED422407)

Carr, M., & Borkowski, J. (1987). Metamemory in gifted children. *Gifted Child Quarterly, 31(1)*, 40–44.

Clark, B. (1988). *Growing up gifted: Developing the potential of children at home and at school* (3rd ed.). Upper Saddle River, NJ: Merrill Publishing.

Clark, B. (1997). Social ideologies and gifted education in today's schools. *Peabody Journal of Education, 72(3&4)*, 81–100.

Coleman, M. R. (2003). *The identification of students who are gifted*. Arlington, VA: ERIC Clearinghouse on Disabilities and Gifted Education. (ERIC Document Reproduction Service No. ED480431)

Cotton, K. (1988). *Classroom questioning*. Portland, OR: Northwest Regional Educational Laboratory. Retrieved August 31, 2006, from http://www.nwrel.org/scpd/sirs/3/cu5.html

Davis, G. (1998). *Creativity is forever*. Dubuque, IA: Kendall/Hunt Publishing.

DeLisle, J. (2000). Once upon a mind: The stories and scholars of gifted child education. Fort Worth, TX: Harcourt Brace.

Fillippone, M. (1998). *Questioning at the elementary level.* Unpublished master's thesis, Kean University, Union, New Jersey. (ERIC Document Reproduction Service No. ED417431)

Gardner, H. (1983). *Frames of mind: The theory of multiple intelligences.* New York: Basic Books.

Gardner, H. (1995). Reflections on multiple intelligences: Myths and messages. *Phi Delta Kappan, 77(3),* 200–203, 206–209.

Gardner, H. (2003, April). *Multiple intelligences after twenty years.* Paper presented at the American Educational Research Association, Chicago, Illinois.

Giftedness and the gifted: What's it all about? (1990). Reston, VA: ERIC Clearinghouse on Handicapped and Gifted Children. (ERIC Document Reproduction Service No. ED321481)

Guskey, T. (2001, April). *Benjamin S. Bloom's contribution to curriculum, instruction, and school learning.* Paper presented at the annual meeting of the American Educational Research Association, Seattle, Washington. (ERIC Document Reproduction Service No. ED457185)

Hamaker, C. (1986). The effects of adjunct questions on prose learning. *Review of Educational Research, 56(2),* 212–242.

Heacox, D. (2001). *Differentiating instruction in the regular classroom: How to reach and teach all learners, grades 3–12.* Minneapolis, MN: Free Spirit Publishing.

Hoge, R. D., & Renzulli, J. S. (1991). *Self-concept and the gifted child* (Research-Based Decision Making Series, No. 9104). Storrs, CT: National Research Center on the Gifted and Talented. (ERIC Document Reproduction Service No. ED358661)

Inman, T., & Roberts, J. (2006, Winter). Differentiation tips for teachers: Practical strategies for the classroom, Part 2: Content, process, product. *The Challenge No. 16,* 12 & 14. Retrieved October 11, 2006, from http://www.wku.edu/gifted/Challenge16.pdf

Kaplan, S. N. (2005). Layering differentiated curriculum for the gifted and talented. In F. A. Karnes & S. M. Bean (Eds.), *Methods and materials for teaching the gifted* (2nd ed., pp. 107–131). Waco, TX: Prufrock Press.

Kingore, B. (2006). Tiered instruction: Beginning the process. *Teaching for High Potential* (Winter). Retrieved September 3, 2006, from the NAGC Website: http://www.nagc.org/CMS400Min/index.aspx?id=1488

Kirchner, J., & Inman, T. (2005). Differentiation tips for teachers: Practical strategies for the classroom, Part I: Preassessment. *The Challenge No. 14*, 10–11. Retrieved October 10, 2006, from http://www.wku.edu/gifted/Challenge14.pdf

Lovecky, D. V. (1992). Exploring social and emotional aspects for giftedness in children. *Roeper Review 15(1)*, 18–25.

Marland, S. P. (1971). *Education of the gifted and talented*. Washington, DC: U.S. Government Printing Office.

Mueller, D. E. (1972). Teacher questioning practices in reading. *Reading World, 12(2)*, 136–145.

National Advisory Committee on Creative and Cultural Education. (1999, May). *All our futures: Creativity, culture and education*. Report to the Secretary of State for Education and Employment and the Secretary of State for Culture, Media, and Sport.

National Association for Gifted Children. (1994). *Differentiation of curriculum and instruction* (Position paper). Retrieved August 28, 2006, from http://www.nagc. org/index.aspx?id=387

National Association for Gifted Children. (2005a). *The history of gifted and talented education*. Retrieved August 26, 2006, from http://www.nagc.org/index. aspx?id=607

National Association for Gifted Children. (2005b). *What is gifted?* Retrieved August 26, 2006, from http://www.nagc.org/index.aspx?id=574&ir

No Child Left Behind Act of 2001, 20 U.S.C. § 7801 *et seq.*

Osborn, A. F. (1963). *Applied imagination: Principles and procedures of creative problem solving* (3rd ed.). New York: Scribner's.

Parke, B. N. (1989). *Gifted students in regular classrooms*. Boston: Allyn & Bacon.

Pressley, M., Wood, E., Woloshyn, V. E., Martin, V., King, A., & Menke, D. (1992). Encouraging mindful use of prior knowledge: Attempting to construct explanatory answers facilitates learning. *Educational Psychologist, 27(1)*, 91–109.

Reis, S. M. (2004). *Self-regulated learning and academically talented students.* Retrieved September 4, 2006, from the NAGC Website: http://www.nagc.org/CMS400Min/index.aspx?id=380

Reis, S. M., & Renzulli, J. S. (1992). Using curriculum compacting to challenge the above-average. *Educational Leadership, 50(2)*, 51–57.

Reis, S. M., Burns, D. E., & Renzulli, J. S. (1992). *Curriculum compacting: The complete guide to modifying the regular curriculum for high ability students.* Mansfield Center, CT: Creative Learning Press.

Reis, S. M., Westberg, K. L., Kulikowich, J., Caillard, F., Hébert, T., Plucker, J., Purcell, J. H., Rogers, J., & Smist, J. (1993). *Why not let high ability students start school in January? The curriculum compacting study* (Research Monograph 93106). Storrs, CT: The National Research Center on the Gifted and Talented, University of Connecticut. (ERIC Document Reproduction Service No. ED379847)

Renzulli, J. S. (1994). *Schools for talent development: A practical plan for total school improvement.* Mansfield Center, CT: Creative Learning Press.

Renzulli, J. S. (1995). *Building a bridge between gifted education and total school improvement* (Talent Development Research-Based Decision Making Series No. 9502). Storrs, CT: National Research Center on the Gifted and Talented, University of Connecticut. (ERIC Document Reproduction Service No. ED388013)

Renzulli, J. S., & Reis, S. M. (1985). *The schoolwide enrichment model: A comprehensive plan for educational excellence.* Mansfield Center, CT: Creative Learning Press.

Renzulli, J. S., & Reis, S. M. (1996). The schoolwide enrichment model: New directions for developing high-end learning. In N. Colangelo & G. A. Davis (Eds.), *Handbook of gifted education* (2nd ed., pp. 136–154). Boston: Allyn & Bacon.

Renzulli, J. S. , & Smith, L. H. (1978). *The compactor.* Mansfield Center, CT: Creative Learning Press.

Rogers, K. B. (1986). Do the gifted think and learn differently? A review of recent research and its implications for instruction. *Journal for the Education of the Gifted, 10(1)*, 17–39.

Runco, M. A. (1986). Maximal performance on divergent thinking tests by gifted, talented, and nongifted children. *Psychology in the Schools, 23(3)*, 308–315.

Smutney, J. F. (2000). *Teaching young gifted children in the regular classroom.* Reston, VA: ERIC Clearinghouse on Disabilities and Gifted Education. (ERIC Document Reproduction Service No. ED445422)

Tomlinson, C. A. (1995). *Differentiating instruction for advanced learners in the mixed-ability middle school classroom.* Reston, VA: ERIC Clearinghouse on Disabilities and Gifted Education. (ERIC Document Reproduction Service No. ED389141)

Tomlinson, C. A. (1997). *The dos and don'ts of instruction: What it means to teach gifted learners well.* Retrieved September 8, 2006, from the NAGC Website: http://www.nagc.org/CMS400Min/index.aspx?id=659

Tomlinson, C. A. (1999). Mapping a route toward differentiated instruction. *Educational Leadership, 57(1)*, 12–16.

Tomlinson, C. A. (2001). *How to differentiate instruction in mixed-ability classrooms* (2nd ed.). Alexandria, VA: Association for Supervision and Curriculum Development.

Torrance, P. E. (1986). Teaching creative and gifted learners. In M. C. Wittrock (Ed.), *Handbook of research on teaching* (3rd ed., pp. 630–647). New York: MacMillan.

Wallas, G. (1926*). The art of thought.* New York: Harcourt Brace.

Winebrenner, S. (1992). *Teaching gifted kids in the regular classroom.* Minneapolis, MN: Free Spirit Publishing.

Winebrenner, S., & Berger, S. (1994). *Providing curriculum alternatives to motivate gifted students.* Reston, VA: ERIC Clearinghouse on Disabilities and Gifted Education. (ERIC Reproduction Service No. ED372553)

Winner, E. (1996). *Gifted children: Myths and realities.* New York: Basic Books.

VanTassel-Baska, J. (1992). *Developing learner outcomes for gifted students.* Reston, VA: ERIC Clearinghouse on Handicapped and Gifted Children. (ERIC Document Reproduction Service No. ED352775)

Notes

Notes